HOW TO BECOME A
PSNI POLICE OFFICER

www.How2Become.com

Orders: Please contact How2become Ltd, Suite 2, 50 Churchill Square Business Centre, Kings Hill, Kent ME19 4YU.

You can order through Amazon.co.uk under ISBN 978-1-910602-23-2, via the website www.How2Become. com or through Gardners.com.

ISBN: 978-1-910602-23-2

First published in 2015 by How2become Ltd.

Typeset for How2become Ltd by Anton Pshinka.
Printed in Great Britain for How2become Ltd by:
CMP (uk) Limited, Poole, Dorset.

Disclaimer

Every effort has been made to ensure that the information contained within this guide is accurate at the time of publication. How2become Ltd are not responsible for anyone failing any part of any selection process as a result of the information contained within this guide. How2become Ltd and their authors cannot accept any responsibility for any errors or omissions within this guide, however caused. No responsibility for loss or damage occasioned by any person acting, or refraining from action, as a result of the material in this publication can be accepted by How2become Ltd.

The information within this guide does not represent the views of any third party service or organisation.

CONTENTS

INTRODUCTION

to your New Guide

Welcome to How To Become a PSNI Police Officer: The Insider's Guide. This guide has been designed to help you prepare for and pass the tough PSNI selection process. PSNI stands for **Police Service of Northern Ireland**. The police force of Northern Ireland are an integral part of community safety, and play a valuable role in upholding justice and peace within the country.

The selection process to join the PSNI is highly competitive. In the last few years, over 7,500 people have applied to join the service every year. Only around 500 of these applicants will be successful; with 100 being accepted on an initial basis and the other spots going to officers who have been placed on the merit list. You could view this as a worrying statistic, or alternatively you could make it your mission to be one of the successful applicants. Armed with our insider's guide, you have already taken the first step to passing the PSNI selection process.

The guide itself has been split up into useful sections to make it easier for you to prepare for each stage of the selection process. Read each section carefully and take notes as you progress. Don't ever give up on your dreams; if you really want to become a PSNI police officer, then you can do it. The best way to approach the selection process is to embark on a programme of 'in-depth' preparation, and this guide will show you exactly how to do that!

In order to pass the police officer selection process, you will need to develop your own skills and experience in terms of the core competencies required to become a police officer. Many candidates who apply to join the service will be unaware that these core competencies even exist. As you progress through this guide, you will find that these elements form the foundations of your preparation. Having a clear understanding of the expectations required, will undoubtedly improve your overall performance during the selection process. With this in mind, the first step of your preparation should be to gain access to a copy of the police officer core competencies. These will usually be a part of your application pack, but if they aren't, you can obtain a copy of them by visiting the website of the service that you are applying for.

If you need any further help with any elements of the police officer selection process, including role plays, written tests and interviews, then we offer a wide range of products to assist you. These products are all available through our website, www.how2become.com. We also run a 1-day intensive Police Officer Course. This will be extremely useful if you are applying to become a PSNI officer, as the majority of the requirements and competencies are very similar. Details of our 1-day course are available at the following website: www.policecourse.co.uk.

We hope you enjoy this professional guide and find it a useful tool to guide you through the initial stages of the selection process. We wish you every success in your pursuit to becoming a PSNI police officer.

If you work hard, and stay focused, you can achieve anything that you set your mind to!

Best wishes,

The how2become team

The How2become Team

CHAPTER 1

How to Pass the
PSNI Police Officer
Selection Process

Before we move on to the different stages of the PSNI selection process, it is important to explain both the core competencies and the key behaviours that are expected of an officer within the service.

Let's break down the key preparation areas in order to enhance your knowledge regarding the role of a PSNI police officer:

THE ROLE:

Prior to completing the first stage of the application process, it is essential that you learn about the role of a police officer. There are two reasons for this. Firstly, you need to be 100% certain that this is the right career choice for you. I know several people who have joined the service, only to leave a few months later because *'it wasn't what they expected'*. The second reason is that prior knowledge about the role is crucial if you wish to successfully pass each stage of the selection process. The better your understanding of what the process will entail, the better your chances of success. Preparation is also crucial to your success. Without making the most of your preparation time, it is unlikely that you will pass. Therefore, we suggest that you take full advantage of the time that you have to prepare for the process.

There are a huge number of ways that you can learn about the role. To begin with, you will find lots of useful information in this guide. You'll also find plenty of information on the PSNI website, and there will inevitably be a wealth of other resources online at your disposal.

When reading this guide, and visiting these websites, take notes on the information that you learn about the role. This will enable you to gain an in-depth understanding of the role, and in turn will make the selection process far easier to pass.

CORE COMPETENCIES:

The PSNI police officer core competencies are the basic skills that a police officer must be able to master if he or she is to be 'capable' of successfully performing the role. Throughout this guide, I will make continued reference to these competencies. I cannot emphasise how important they are. During the selection process, you will be assessed against these core competencies at every stage; therefore it is essential that you are able to learn, understand and demonstrate them in every stage of the application process.

It is important that you obtain a copy of the police officer core competencies prior to completing the application form. You will need to match these essential competencies when filling out your application form. If you are unable to demonstrate these skills, your application form is likely to be rejected, and you will not be able to progress to the next stage of the selection process. You will also use the core competencies during your preparation for the assessment centre and also the final interview, if applicable.

As you can see, the first step on the road to passing the police officer selection process is to learn as much as possible about the role. On the following pages you will find brief details about the role and your training. This should be used as a guideline only. You should check the PSNI website for the most relevant and up to date details on the job for which you are applying.

The great thing about life as a police officer is that you have the ability to make a difference. On many occasions, your actions will be able to change people's lives. It is a demanding but highly satisfying career, which will ultimately provide you with the opportunity to make a difference to your community. You will face challenges on a daily basis, but your training will provide you with the essential tools and skills to overcome these difficulties in a professional and effective manner. Working in the police service provides the opportunity to perform a wide range of roles and to take personal responsibility for helping others. Dignity and respect are key elements of a police officer's working life. There is no greater feeling than bringing offenders to justice. Unfortunately, for every offender there will be at least one victim, and an arrest means nothing if justice is not delivered in court. As a police officer, you can ensure that justice is delivered by carrying out your job competently, following the correct policies and procedures, and filing accurate and concise paperwork.

With this in mind, it is important to remember that you are there to serve the public. Foremost, you hold a position in the community where people will look to you for support, security and safeguarding. Life as a police officer is not all about catching and convicting criminals. You must have the community's best interests at heart, and you will be assessed against how well you can assert yourself in terms of community values during your selection process. Duties of a police officer can include patrolling on foot or in cars, investigating crime scenes, attending incidents, and interacting with the members of your community. At times, this can be emotionally taxing. You need to ensure that you are prepared for this side of the role.

For example, you might be given the challenging task of telling a mother or father that their child has been injured or killed in a road accident. You will need to conduct yourself in a compassionate and professional manner, in order to provide the most effective service.

During my career in the Fire Service, I attended many incidents where a member of the public had sadly lost their life. I did not envy the police officers that had the task of breaking this bad news to families of the victims. In order to carry out this part of the role, you will need to possess great courage and sensitivity. There will also be times when you need to sit down and work on the administrative side of the role, and will be required to spend time giving evidence in court.

As you can see, the role of a PSNI police officer varies somewhat on a day-to-day basis. You will face different tasks and scenarios every day, each requiring a different approach. If you believe that you have what it takes to deal with these challenges, then this job could be perfect for you.

Finally, you should also be prepared for physical conditions, such as spending long hours on the beat in extremely cold weather. Your fitness levels must be adequate enough to withstand the demanding nature of the job. One of the most common reasons that candidates are rejected from the PSNI is due to their lack of physical fitness.

Whilst the physical tests are not particularly difficult, you must prepare well for them. You can improve your fitness levels by undergoing a period of intense preparation and training. Here at how2become, we provide fitness tools to help you with this fitness training. For further details, please visit our website www.how2become.com to find out more on the types of fitness products that are available.

OPPORTUNITIES FOR PROGRESSION:

If you are good at your job, and are a motivated and ambitious person, then there will certainly be many opportunities for promotion within the service. The police service will always need officers on the beat, but they will also need managers who are capable of driving the organisation forward. Everyone in the service has an equal opportunity for promotion, so if you are keen and enthusiastic, then there's nothing to stop you from reaching the top!

Furthermore, the PSNI also runs a High Potential Development Scheme, which provides fast-track opportunities for individuals who can demonstrate the right level of potential. This scheme is open to everyone, and is based upon merit. If you work hard, you will be rewarded!

THE WORKING WEEK:

A normal working week for a police officer consists of 40 hours, divided up on a shift-basis. The shift pattern that you will normally work forms part of your contract, and these can vary between each police service. All of the ranks below superintendent will be given two rest days each week, and compensation will be given if you ever have to work during those two days. If you want to know more about the different types of shift pattern, then you should contact your local constabulary.

We have now covered a number of important aspects of a police officer's role. During your preparation, don't forget to visit the PSNI website, and also read further recruitment literature in order to gain an in-depth knowledge of the service. If I was to ask you, 'what can you tell me about the role of a police officer?' would you be able to answer it effectively?

In the next chapter, I'll give you my top 10 insider's tips to assist you during your preparation for becoming a police officer.

CHAPTER 2

Insider Tips and Advice

The following tips have been carefully thought out, in the hopes of increasing your chances of success during the PSNI police officer selection process. Therefore, it is important that you follow them carefully. Whilst some of them will appear obvious, many applicants fail to remember them. It is important to use these tips and insights as a way of tailoring your preparation, to increase your overall performance and to enhance your chances of a successful application.

BE PREPARED:

Regardless of the career for which you are applying, it is vitally important that you prepare yourself fully for every stage of the process. Make sure that you read every single bit of information that you have been given, at least twice, and fully understand what it is that you will be required to do to pass. Go out of your way to prepare. For example, get a friend or relative to act out a role-play scenario to see how you deal with it. Let them give you feedback on your performance, and use that feedback as a way of improving your performance.

When completing the application form, make sure that you allocate plenty of time to do it neatly, concisely and correctly. Don't leave it until the night before to fill out the form. In addition to your preparation, it is also very important to believe in your own abilities and take advantage of your potential. For example, if you have applied to the PSNI previously and failed, what have you done to improve your chances of success the second time around? Did you work out what areas you failed in, and have you done anything to improve them?

I would recommend that you structure your preparation time, in order to focus on different stages of the selection process. I often organise my time by using a timetable, and spend half an hour/to an hour researching, preparing and practising different areas of the application process. For example, on Monday, you might spend half an hour researching the role of a police officer and then spend an hour drafting your responses to the questions on your application form. Remember to mix this up! Spend time on your weakest areas, to ensure your performance is well-rounded.

DEMONSTRATE YOUR VALUES:

One of the key aspects of working as a police officer, is behaving with dignity and respect. If you do not believe in equality, fairness and dignity, then you are applying for the wrong job. You'll be expected to demonstrate all of these to a high standard during the selection process. Police officers are role models within society and people will look to you to set an example. You wouldn't expect to see a police officer bullying or shouting at a member of the public, would you? As a police officer, you should only use force in exceptional circumstances. You will have to use your interpersonal skills to diffuse difficult situations, and you will need to treat people fairly and equally at all times. During the selection process, your understanding and knowledge of equality and fairness will be tested via the application form, the written tests and during the interview and role-play scenarios. You'll be required to demonstrate that you have a good respect for race and diversity, and that you believe in equal opportunities for everyone.

PHYSICAL AND MENTAL FITNESS:

If you are to be successful in your application as a police officer, it is important that you are both physically and mentally fit. In addition to benefitting your health, being physically fit will also improve your self-esteem and confidence. Equally as important are the benefits of having 'a healthy mind', which will help you to learn new skills, and develop old ones. The fitter your mind, the easier this will be.

Furthermore, if you are both physically and mentally fit, then you will be able to prepare for longer. You will find that your stamina levels increase, and so will your ability to practice. Make sure you get plenty of sleep in the build up to the assessment day, and ensure that you eat a healthy balanced diet. You will find that if you spend just a week or two eating and drinking the right things, then you will begin to look and feel healthier. Avoid junk food, alcohol and cigarettes during your preparation, to ensure that your concentration levels are at their best.

LEARN ABOUT THE PSNI:

Spending an adequate amount of time learning about the PSNI selection process is hugely important for a number of reasons. Firstly, on the application form, you might be asked a question that relates to your knowledge of the role and why you want to join the PSNI. As you can appreciate, they want to know exactly what it is about them that attracts you to the job. In order to provide a good response to this type of question, you will need to carry out some research.

One of the best ways to gain this information is to visit the PSNI website, and find out ways that they are helping the community. If you come into the process with a prior knowledge of the service and what they have to offer, then you will demonstrate enthusiasm and commitment towards the cause. Telling an interview panel about current crime trends, statistics and local policing issues in your area, will highlight the time and effort that you have put in to prepare for the assessment. This will go a long way to helping you gain a position in the service.

If you were interviewing a candidate for employment, think about what you would expect them to know. Would you expect them to have undertaken a great deal of research beforehand? If they did have a large amounts of prior knowledge, how would you judge them against someone who didn't? You should always attempt to learn as much information as possible about the force, and be extremely thorough in your preparation.

CORE COMPETENCIES:

The police officer core competencies identify how you should behave and perform whilst employed within the service. It is **absolutely fundamental** that you have a strong knowledge of all of the competencies required before you start the application process. They are crucial to your success. Throughout the process you should concentrate on demonstrating the core competencies at every single stage; from your initial application form all the way through to the final assessments.

The most effective way to achieve this is to use keywords and phrases in your responses to the application form and interview questions. You can also adopt this method when tackling your role-plays and written tests. Using words that correspond with these competencies will improve your scores and give you a better chance of being successful. When you are filling in your application forms and preparing for the assessment centre, always make sure that you have a copy of the competencies next to you. These competencies cover a wide range of skills; such as customer focused, problem solving and team work. As we have mentioned, you should be able to find these on any employer's website. In chapter 3, we have provided you with detailed information on all of the PSNI core competencies.

BE PATIENT AND LEARN FROM YOUR MISTAKES:

As we have highlighted, the police force receive thousands of applications each year, and it takes time to process each one. While you are waiting for them to get in touch with you, use your time wisely and concentrate on the next stage of the selection process.

Once you have submitted your application form, start immediate work on your preparation for the assessment centre. The overwhelming majority of candidates will not start their preparation until they receive their results, and as a consequence will miss out on an extra few weeks valuable practice time. You are applying to join a job which will pay you approximately £30,000 a year, what more reason do you need to study? Use every bit of your spare time to prepare for the next stage.

If you have previously been through the selection process, and failed, then you need to find out why you failed. You should always receive a feedback form from the police force informing you of which areas you need to improve upon. There is no point going through the selection process again if you are just going to make the same mistakes.

UNDERSTANDING DIVERSITY:

It is fundamentally important that the police force represents the community that it serves. British communities are diversifying at a furious rate, and the best way to deal with this is to have a multi-cultural police force. Ask yourself the question, 'what is diversity?'

If you cannot answer then you will need to find out. Both the application form and final interview will test your knowledge of diversity and multi-culturalism. Remember that as a police officer, you must uphold the law fairly in order to protect, respect and help everyone in the community. You must also meet with current legislative requirements concerning human rights, race, disability and equality.

An ability to demonstrate a wide understanding of diversity will be vitally important during the selection process, and will be even more important when you are working as a police officer.

NEVER GIVE UP:

If you don't succeed at the first attempt, don't give up. As long as you are constantly improving, there is always a chance that you will succeed. The best way to do this is to look at the stages you have failed and work hard at improving your ability. Don't just sit back and wait for the next opportunity, prepare for it straight away and you'll increase your chances for next time. Too many people give up on their goals far too easily. Learning to find the positive aspects in negative situations is a difficult thing to do, but is a skill that anyone can acquire through practice and determination. If you really want to achieve your goals, then anything is possible.

During your preparation, set yourself small targets every week. For example, your first week may be used to concentrate on learning the core competencies, and the second week could be used to prepare for your written responses on the application form. Don't underestimate the value of breaks. If you feel tired or de-motivated at any time, walk away and give yourself some time off. You may find that you come back to the task re-energised, more focused and determined to succeed.

PRACTICE ROLE-PLAYS:

The role-play can be particularly daunting, especially if you have never done anything like it before. Whilst you are encouraged to be yourself, there are many ways in which you can prepare yourself and increase your chances of success.

The best way to prepare for the role-play exercises is to act them out in a room with a friend or relative. Further on in this guide, we have provided you with a number of example role-play scenarios. The only way that you will be able to understand what is required during the role-play is to understand the core competencies that are being assessed.

For example, if you are being assessed on your customer-focus skills, then you will need to demonstrate the following during each role-play scenario:

• Presenting a professional and appropriate image that is in line with your brief and job description;

- A complete focus on the needs of the customer;

- A swift and efficient attitude to problem solving, and a sincere apology to the customer for any mistakes that have been made. This includes ensuring that the customer is satisfied with the result of your actions, and if not, taking alternative steps to satisfy their needs.

PRACTICE A MOCK INTERVIEW:

Mock interviews are a fantastic way to prepare for both the assessment centre interview, and also the final interview.

During the build up to previous interviews, I made a habit of writing down predicted interview questions that I had created for my research. I would then ask a friend or relative to ask me these questions under formal interview conditions. I found this to be excellent preparation, and it certainly served me well during all of my career interviews. I would estimate that I was successful at over 90% of all of the interviews I attended. I put this success purely down to my detailed preparation.

Finally, I also recommend sitting down in front of a mirror and responding to the same set of interview questions. Study your interview technique. Do you slouch? Do you fidget, and do you overuse your hands? It is hugely important that you work on your interview technique during the build-up to your interviews. If you have prepared fully, you will be amazed at how confident you will feel during the actual interview.

In the next section of the guide, we'll give you a detailed insight into the best way to complete the PSNI application form. We'll show you what questions to expect, how to answer them, and how to ensure that your application form exhibits all of the core competencies that the police force are looking for, which will ultimately put your application miles in front of other candidates.

CHAPTER 3

*How to Complete
the Application Form*

The application form is the first stage of the selection process for becoming a PSNI police officer. During this section, I will provide you with a step-by-step approach to completing a successful application. It is important to point out that I have used a number of the more common types of application form question within this section, and therefore it is your responsibility to confirm that they are related to your particular form. When completing your application form, I would recommend that you allow at least five evenings to complete the form, breaking it up into manageable sections. Many candidates will try and complete the form in one sitting, and as a result the quality of their submission will suffer.

On the following pages, I have provided you with tips and advice on how to approach a number of different questions. Please remember that these are provided as a guideline only, and that you should base your answers around your own experiences in both your work and personal life. Many of the questions will require you to demonstrate that you have the knowledge, skills and experience as outlined by the personal specification of the job that you are applying for. Therefore, your answers should match these qualities as closely as possible.

Your first step should be to study the personal specification of the role. As we have mentioned, the role of a police officer is essentially made up of a number of core competencies. You'll find these in your application pack, or on the PSNI website. Always make sure that you have a copy of these next to you when you are completing the form, as you will need to match your responses with them. The core competencies that form the basis of a police officer role are as follows:

PUBLIC SERVICE:

This requires a candidate to demonstrate a genuine belief in good public service, focusing on what matters to the public and serving the best interests of the community. You will need to understand the expectations and varying needs of different communities, and take steps to address them. You'll need to build good relationships with people in the community by talking to them and exploring their viewpoints. Finally, you will be required to show an understanding of the impact and benefits that policing can have on different communities, and identify the best way to deliver service to the public. This can often involve working in partnership with other agencies.

ADAPTABILITY:

This requires a candidate to demonstrate openness and positivity towards change, and to be able to adapt rapidly to different ways of working. You will need a flexible and open approach towards alternative methods of solving problems, and will be required to show an innovative and creative attitude towards finding and executing new solutions.

SERVICE DELIVERY:

This requires a candidate to show a wider understanding of the organisation's objectives and priorities, and identify how their own work fits into these. You'll need to plan and organise tasks, and take a structured approach to solving problems.

You'll also be expected to manage multiple tasks, and show advanced thought processes when prioritising and managing these activities. Your focus should be on the end result of the task, with the aim of working efficiently and accurately to achieve the best possible service for the customer.

PROFESSIONALISM:

As a police officer, it is vital that you are professional and act with integrity at all times. You must take ownership for resolving problems, display courage and resilience when faced with challenging situations, and act on your own initiative to address potential issues. You'll need to act honestly and ethically, and challenge any conduct or behaviour that you identify as being out of line with the ethical values of the police service. Finally, you'll need to display a calm and professional attitude when you are under pressure, and must be prepared to step forward and defuse conflict in difficult scenarios.

DECISION MAKING:

Decision making is extremely important for police officers. It is vital that you are able to make appropriate and unbiased judgements, to gain an accurate understanding of situations. You'll need to weigh up a range of possible options, before making clear and justifiable decisions. You'll also be required to review your original decisions, in the light of new information and changing circumstances. All of your decisions and actions should be in the best interests of the public.

WORKING WITH OTHERS:

It is really important as a police officer that you have the ability to work co-operatively with others. You'll need to be approachable, positive, a great listener and a great communicator. You should demonstrate that you are someone who can persuade people, keep them informed and display a compassionate and empathic attitude to their situation. You will need to treat all people with respect, fairness and dignity, regardless of their background or circumstances.

Now that we have taken a brief look at some of the core competencies, we can start to look at some of the application form questions.

Before we do this, take a read of the following important tips, which will help you to submit a first class application:

- Make sure that you read the whole of the application form at least twice before preparing your responses, including the guidance notes;

- Read and understand the person specification and the police officer core competencies;

- Try to tailor your answers around the 'core competencies' and include any keywords or phrases that you think are relevant;

- Make sure that you base your answers on actual events that you have experienced either in your work life or personal life;

- Make sure that you fill out the form in the correct ink colour. If you fail to follow this simple instruction, then your form may end up in the bin;

- If there is a specific word count for each question, make sure that you stick to it;

- Make sure that you keep a photocopy of your completed application form before sending it off, as you could be asked questions relating to it during the interview stage;

- Get someone to read your completed application form to check for spelling/grammar mistakes;

- Answer all of the questions to the best of your ability. If you leave a question blank, it is highly unlikely that you will move on to the next stage;

- Use examples from your work, social, domestic or educational life to answer the questions. In these examples, they are looking for evidence of specific behaviours or skills which are essential to police work;

- Be specific: they want to know what YOU said or did to deal with a particular situation. It's important that you provide examples of your own experiences, and provide clear details about the situation that you encountered;

- Write clearly and concisely. The PSNI will expect your answers to be focused, succinct and fluently written, just like any police report or statement would need to be. This means writing in complete sentences, rather than in notes or bullet points;

- Pay attention to your handwriting, spelling, punctuation and grammar. Remember that this is a formal application so the use of jargon and slang is unacceptable;

- Finally, send your application form via recorded delivery. This will prevent your form from going missing in the post, which happens more often than you might think.

SAMPLE APPLICATION FORM QUESTIONS AND RESPONSES:

The following sample application form questions will provide you with some excellent tips and advice on how to approach the questions. While you may not necessarily encounter the exact same questions, you are likely to see very similar questions, and this will help you to prepare and plan your answers in advance.

Sample question number 1

'What knowledge, skills and experiences do you have that will enable you to meet the requirements of a police officer?'

ANSWER:

"In my previous role as a customer service assistant, I was required to work closely with the general public. Often I was required to provide varied solutions to customer's problems or complaints. It was always important for me to listen carefully to what they had to say and respond in a manner that was both respectful and understanding.

On some occasions I would have to communicate with members of the public from a different race or background. I paid particular attention to helping them understand exactly how I was going to resolve their problems. I was always sensitive to the way in which they might have been feeling. Every Monday morning, my team would hold a meeting to discuss the ways in which we could improve our customer service. During these meetings, I would always ensure that I contributed and shared any relevant personal experiences from the previous week. Sometimes during the group discussions I would find that certain members of the group were shy and not very confident at coming forward, so I sensitively tried to involve them wherever possible.

On one occasion, during a meeting, I provided a solution to a problem that had been on-going for some time. I had noticed that customers would often call back to see if their complaint had been resolved, which was time-consuming for the company to deal with. I suggested that we should have a system where customers were called back after 48 hours with an update of progress in relation to their complaint. My suggestion was taken forward and is now an integral part of the company's procedures. I found it quite hard at first to persuade managers to take on my idea, but I was confident that the change would provide a better service to the public."

Using the answer that we have provided, try to 'match' the answer to the core competencies that are relevant to the role of a police officer.

For example, the first paragraph reads as follows:

"In my previous role as a customer service assistant I was required to work closely with the general public. Often I was required to provide varied solutions to customer's problems or complaints. It was always important for me to listen carefully to what they had to say and respond in a manner that was both respectful and understanding."

This answer matches elements of the core competencies of **public service**. Now, take a look at the next paragraph.

"On some occasions I would have to communicate with members of the public from a different race or background. I paid particular attention to helping them understand exactly how I was going to resolve their problems. I was always sensitive to the way in which they might have been feeling."

This response matches elements of the core competency of **working with others.** Hopefully you are now beginning to understand what is required and how important it is to 'match' your response with the core competencies that are being assessed. Remember to make sure you read the guidance notes that are contained within your application pack. Once you do, you will start to realise why I recommend that you set aside five evenings to complete the form!

When using examples, don't just think about your work experiences, but look at other aspects of your life too. Try to think of any community work that you have been involved in. Have you ever been a special constable, or do you work for a charity or neighbourhood watch? If so, you should find it fairly simple to match your competencies with those required by the employer.

I have now provided a number of sample keywords and phrases that are relevant to each core competency. These will help you to understand exactly what I mean when I say 'match' the core competencies in each of your responses. You might consider using these keywords and phrases in your responses to the application form questions, and other elements of the police officer selection process.

PUBLIC SERVICE:

- Focused on the customer at all times to ensure that I delivered an excellent service;

- I addressed the needs of the person I was dealing with;

- I listened to their viewpoint;

- By speaking with them, I was able to build their confidence in my abilities;

- I took the time to identify the best way to meet their needs;

- I worked alongside other people to ensure that the best service was delivered.

OPENNESS TO CHANGE:

- I was positive about making changes;

- I took steps to adapt to the new working-practices;

- I put in extra effort to make the changes work;

- I was flexible in my approach to work;

- I searched for alternative ways to deal with the situation;

- I took an innovative approach to working with the new guidelines and procedures.

SERVICE DELIVERY:

- I consider the organisation's main objectives and aims whilst carrying out my work;

- Used an action plan to help me achieve the task;

- I was organised in my approach to the working situation;

- I managed a number of different tasks at once and ensured that my time-management was effective;

- I focused at all times on the end result;

- I asked for clarification whenever I was unsure.

PROFESSIONALISM:

- I acted professionally and ethically at all times;

- I took responsibility for solving the problem;

- I stood by my decision despite the objections from others;

- I remained calm at all times and in control of the situation;

- I immediately challenged the inappropriate behaviour;

- In order to improve my performance, I sought feedback from my manager;

- I took steps to defuse the conflict;

- I took control of the situation in order to achieve a positive outcome.

DECISION MAKING:

- I gathered all of the information available before making my decision;

- I verified that the information was accurate before using it to make a decision;

- I considered all possible options first;
- I reviewed my decision once the new information had become available;
- I considered the wider implications before making my decision;
- I remained impartial at all times;
- I considered the confidentiality of the information I was receiving.

WORKING WITH OTHERS:

- I worked with the other members of the team to get the task completed;
- At all times, I considered the other members of the team and offered my support whenever possible;
- I took steps to develop a positive working relationship with the other members of the team;
- I fully briefed the other members of the team on what we needed to achieve;
- I adapted my style of communication to fit the audience;
- I listened to other people's views and took them into consideration;
- I took positive steps to persuade the team to follow my course of action;
- I kept the others updated of my progress at all times;
- I addressed their needs and concerns immediately;
- At all times, I treated others with respect and dignity.

You will notice that I have used the word 'I' many times during the above sample keywords and phrases, this is deliberate. Remember, it is important to explain what YOU did during your responses.

Now let's move on to some more sample application form interview questions and responses.

Sample question number 2

'Why have you applied for this post and what do you have to offer?'

"I believe that my personal qualities and attributes would be suited to that of a police officer within the PSNI. I would enjoy the challenge of working in a public service environment that requires a high level of personal responsibility, openness to change and working with others. I have outstanding levels of commitment, motivation and integrity, which I believe would help the Police Force respond to the needs of the community."

The PSNI application form will ask you questions based around the question above. You need to answer in conjunction with the personal specification. When writing your answer to the above question, consider the following information:

- The length of the response that you provide should be dictated by the amount of space available to you on the application form or the specified number of maximum words;

- The form itself may provide you with the facility to attach a separate sheet if necessary. If it doesn't then make sure that you keep to the space provided;

- The best tip that I can give you is to write down your answer first in rough, before committing your answer to paper on the actual application form. This will allow you to iron out any mistakes.

Sample question number 3

'It is essential that police officers are capable of showing respect for other people, regardless of their background. Please describe a situation where you have challenged bullying, discriminatory or insensitive behaviour. You will be assessed on how positively you acted during the situation, and also on how well you understood what had occurred.'

PART 1 – Describe the situation and also tell us about the other person or people who were involved.

"Whilst working as a sales person for my previous employer, I was serving a lady who was from an ethnic background. I was helping her to choose a gift for her son's 7th birthday when a group of four youths entered the shop. They began to make racist jokes and comments to the lady. I was naturally offended by the comments and was concerned for the lady to whom these comments were directed. Any form of bullying and harassment is not welcome, and I was determined to stop it immediately and protect the lady from any more harm."

PART 2 – What did you say and what did you do?

"The lady was clearly upset by their actions and I too found them both offensive and insensitive. I decided to take immediate action and stood between the lady and the group of adolescents, to try to protect her from any more verbal abuse or comments. I told them in a calm manner that their comments were not welcome and would not be tolerated. I then called over my manager for assistance and asked him to call the police before asking the four youths to leave the shop. I wanted to diffuse the situation as soon as possible. I was confident that the shop's CCTV cameras would have picked up the four offending youths and that the police would be able to deal with the situation. After the youths had left the shop, I sat the lady down and made her a cup of tea

whilst we waited for the police to arrive. I did everything that I could to support and comfort the lady and told her that I would be prepared to act as a witness to the bullying and harassment that I had just seen."

PART 3 – Why do you think the other people behaved as they did?

"I believe that their behaviour was predominantly down to a lack of understanding, education and awareness. Unless people are educated and understand why these comments are not acceptable, then they are not open to change. They behave in this manner because they are unaware of how dangerous their comments and actions are. They believe it is socially acceptable to act this way, when it certainly isn't."

PART 4 – What would have been the consequences if you had not acted as you did?

"Well, to begin with I would have been condoning this type of behaviour and missing an opportunity to let the offenders know that their actions were wrong. I would also have let the lady down, which would have in turn made her feel frightened, hurt and unsupported. We all need to help prevent discriminatory behaviour."

- Try to focus your answer on the positive action that you took, identifying that you understood the situation. Don't forget to include keywords and phrases in your response, which are relevant to the competencies being assessed;

- Make sure that you are honest in your responses. The situations that you provide MUST be ones that you have actively taken part in.

- Remember to read the core competencies before constructing your response. What are the police looking for in relation to what YOU say to others and how you act?

- When describing your thoughts or opinions on how others acted in a given situation, keep your personal views separate. Try to provide a response that shows a mature understanding of the situation.

Sample question number 4

"Police officers are required to work in teams and therefore they must be able to work well with others. Please describe a situation where it was necessary to work with other people in order to get something done and achieve a positive result. During this question, you will be assessed on how you cooperated with the other members of the team in order to complete the task at hand."

PART 1 – Tell us what had to be done.

"Whilst driving along the motorway, I noticed that an accident had occurred in front of me. Two cars were involved in the accident and some people in the car appeared to be injured. There were a number of people standing around looking at the crash and I was concerned that help had not been called. We needed to work as a team to call the emergency services, and look after the injured people in the cars."

PART 2 – How was it that you became involved?

"I'm not the type of person to sit in the background and let others resolve situations. I prefer to help out where I can and I believed that, in this situation, something needed to be done. It was apparent that people were hurt and the emergency services had not been called yet. There were plenty of people standing around but they weren't working as a team to help the victims of the crash."

PART 3 – What did you do and what did others do?

"I immediately shouted out loud and asked if anybody was a trained first aid person, nurse or doctor. A man came running

over and told me that he worked for the British Red Cross and that he had a first aid kit in his car. He told me that he would look after the injured people but that he would need an assistant. I asked a nearby lady to help him. I then decided that I needed to call the emergency services and went to use my mobile phone. A man pointed out to me that if I used the orange emergency phone it would get through quicker, and the operator would be able to locate exactly where the accident was. I asked him if he would call the emergency services on his orange phone, as he appeared to know exactly what he was doing. I noticed a lady sat on the embankment next to the hard shoulder crying. She appeared to be in shock. I asked an onlooker if he would sit with her and talk to her until the ambulance got there. Once that was done, the remaining onlookers and I decided to work as a team to remove the debris lying in the road, which would hinder the route for the oncoming emergency service vehicles."

PART 4 – How was it decided which way things were to be done?

"I decided to take the initiative and get everyone working as a team. I asked the people to let me know what their particular strengths were. One person was first aid trained and so he had the task of attending to the injured. Everyone agreed that we needed to work together as a team in order to achieve the task."

PART 5 – What did you do to ensure the team were able to get the result they wanted?

"I took control of a deteriorating situation and got everybody involved. I made sure to ask whether anybody was skilled in certain areas such as first aid and then used the people who had experience, such as the man who knew about the orange emergency telephones. I also kept talking to everybody and asking them if they were OK and happy with what they were doing. I tried my best to co-ordinate the people with jobs that I felt were a priority."

PART 6 – What benefit did your actions have on the situation, and how did the experience benefit you personally?

"The overall benefit was for the injured people, ensuring that they received treatment as soon as possible. However, I did feel a sense of achievement that the team had worked well together even though we had never met each other before. I also learnt a tremendous amount from the experience. At the end we all shook hands and talked briefly and there was a common sense of achievement amongst everybody that we had done something positive. Without each other we wouldn't have been able to get the job done."

- Do not fall into the trap of telling them what you 'would do' if the situation was to occur. Tell them what you DID do;

- It is better to say that you volunteered to get involved, than to say you were asked. This shows initiative;

- Provide a response that is concise and flows in a logical sequence;

- Try to include details that demonstrate how your actions had a positive impact on the result;

Sample question number 5

"During very difficult circumstances, police officers must be able to remain calm and act logically and decisively. Please describe a situation when you have been in a challenging or difficult situation and had to make a decision where other people disagreed with you. You will be assessed on how positively you reacted in the face of adversity."

PART 1 – Tell us about the situation and why you felt it was difficult.

"Whilst working in my current position as a sales person, I was the duty manager for the day as my manager had gone home sick. It was the week before Christmas and the shop was very busy. During the day, the fire alarm went off and I asked everybody to evacuate the shop, which is our company policy. The alarm has gone off in the past, but the normal manager usually lets people stay in the shop whilst he finds out if it's a false alarm. This was a difficult situation because the shop was very busy, nobody wanted to leave and my shop assistants were disagreeing with my decision to evacuate the shop. Some of the customers were irate, as they were in the changing rooms at the time."

PART 2 – Who disagreed with you and what did they say or do?

"Both the customers and my shop assistants were disagreeing with me. The customers were saying that it was appalling that they had to evacuate the shop and that they would complain to the head office about it. The sales staff were trying to persuade me to keep everybody inside the shop and saying that it was most likely a false alarm. I was determined to evacuate everybody from the shop for safety reasons, and would not allow anybody to deter me from my aim. The safety of my staff and customers was at the forefront of my mind."

PART 3 – What did you say or do?

"Whilst remaining calm and in control, I shouted at the top of my voice that everybody needed to leave, despite the sound of the alarm reducing the impact of my voice. I then had to instruct my staff to walk around the shop and tell everybody to leave whilst we investigated the problem. I had to inform one member of staff that disciplinary action would be taken against him if he did not co-operate. Eventually, everybody began to leave the shop. I then went outside with my members of staff, took a roll call and waited for the Fire Brigade to arrive."

PART 4 – Tell us how this situation made you feel.

"At first I felt a little apprehensive and under pressure, but I was determined not to move from my position. I was disappointed that my staff did not initially help me but the more I persisted the more confident I became. This was the first time I had been the manager of the shop so I felt that this situation tested my courage and determination. By remaining calm I was able to deal with the situation far more effectively."

PART 5 – How did you feel immediately after the incident?

"I felt good because I had achieved my aim and I had stood by my decision. It made me feel confident that I could do it again and deal with any difficult situation. I now felt that I had the courage to manage the shop better and had proven to myself that I was capable of dealing with difficult situations. I learned that staying calm under pressure significantly improves your chances of a successful outcome."

- For questions of this nature you will need to focus on the core competency that relates to professionalism. Remember to use keywords and phrases in your responses that match the core competencies being assessed;

- Do not become aggressive or confrontational when dealing with people who disagree with you. Remain calm at all times but be resilient in your actions if it is right to do so;

- Remember to be in control at all times, and remain calm. These are qualities that good police officers will need to possess;

- Do not say that you felt angry and avoid using words that are confrontational;

- By staying calm you will be able to deal with situations far more effectively.

Sample question number 6

"Police officers must deliver an excellent service to the public. It is also important that they build good working relationships with the public and other stakeholders. Describe a situation when you have had to deal with someone who was disappointed with the level of service they received. Try to use an occasion where you had contact with that person over a long period of time, or on a number of different occasions in order to rectify the problem."

PART 1 – Describe the situation and why you think the person was not happy.

"Whilst working as a sales person in my current job, I was approached by an unhappy customer. He explained to me, in an angry manner, that he had bought a pair of running trainers for his daughter's birthday the week before. On the morning of her

birthday, when she unwrapped her present, she noticed that one of the training shoes was a size 6 whilst the other was a size 7. Understandably he was not happy with the level of service that he had received from our company. The reason for his dissatisfaction was that his daughter had been let down on her birthday and as a consequence he then had to travel back into town to sort out a problem that should not have occurred in the first place."

PART 2 – Explain what you did in response to his concerns.

"Immediately I tried to diffuse his anger by telling him that I fully understood his situation and that I would feel exactly the same if I was in his position. I promised him that I would resolve the situation and offered him a cup of tea or coffee whilst he waited for me to address the problem. This appeared to calm him down and the tone of his voice became friendlier. I then spoke to my manager and explained the situation to him. I suggested that maybe it would be a good idea to replace the running shoes with a new pair (both the same size) and also refund the gentleman in full as a gesture to try to make up for our mistake. The manager agreed with my suggestion and so I returned to the gentleman and explained what we proposed to do for him. He was delighted with the offer. We then went over to the checkout to refund his payment and replace the running shoes. At this point, I took down the gentleman's address and telephone number, which is company policy for any goods returned for refund or exchange. The man then left the shop happy with the service he had received. The following day I telephoned the gentleman at home to check that everything was OK with the running shoes and he told me that his daughter was delighted. He also informed me that despite the initial bad experience, he would continue to use our shop in the future."

PART 3 – How did you know that the person was happy with what you did?

"I could detect a change in his behaviour as soon as I explained that I sympathised with his situation. The tone of his voice became less agitated and angry, so I took advantage of this situation and tried even harder to turn his bad experience with us into a positive one. When we offered him the refund along with the replacement of the running shoes he appeared to be extremely satisfied. Finally, when I telephoned him the following day he was so happy that he said he would come back to us again, despite the initial poor level of service."

PART 4 – If you hadn't acted in the way that you did, what do you think the outcome would have been?

"To begin with, I believe the situation would have become even more heated and possibly untenable. His anger or dissatisfaction could have escalated if my attempts to diffuse the situation had not taken place. I also believe that we would have lost a customer and therefore lost future profits for the company. There would have been a high possibility that the gentleman would have taken his complaint higher, either to our head office, trading standards or the local newspaper. Customer service is important and we need to do everything we can (within reason) to make the level of service we provide as high as possible. I also believe that our reputation could have been damaged as that particular gentleman could have told friends or colleagues not to use our shop in the future, whereas now, because of my chosen actions, he would be more inclined to promote us in a positive light instead."

- In order to respond to this type of question accurately, you will need to study and understand the core competency that relates to public service;

- Make sure you answer the question in two parts. Describe the situation and then explain why the person was not happy;

- Remember that public service is an important element of the role of a police officer. You must focus on the needs of the customer or the person you are dealing with at all times;

- In your response to this part of the question, try to indicate that you followed up on your actions by contacting the person, to see if they were satisfied with what you did for them;

- Demonstrate that you have a clear understanding of what would have happened if you had not acted as you did;

- Study the core competency that is relevant to public service before answering this question;

- Use keywords and phrases in your response from the core competency that is being assessed.

Sample question number 7

"Police officers must be organised and manage their own time effectively. Please describe a situation when you were under pressure to carry out a number of tasks at the same time. Tell us what you had to do, which things were a priority and why."

"Whilst working for a sales company as a manager, I had 4 important tasks to complete on the last working day of every month. These tasks included stocktaking reports, approving and submitting the sales reps' mileage claims, auditing the previous month's accounts, and planning the strategy for the following month's activity. My first priority was always to approve and submit the sales reps' mileage claims. If I did not get this right or failed to get them submitted on time, the reps would be out of pocket when they received their payslip. This would in turn affect morale and productivity within the office. The second task to complete would be stocktaking reports. This was important to complete on time, as if I missed the deadline we would not have sufficient stock for the following month, and therefore there would be nothing to sell. This would result in customers not receiving their goods on time. The third task would be the strategy for the following month. This was usually a simple task, but still important, as it would set out my plan for the following month's activities. Finally I would audit the accounts. The reason why I would leave this task until the end is that they did not have to be submitted to Head Office until the 14th day of the month, and therefore I had extra time to complete this task, ensuring that I got it right the first time."

• Try to demonstrate that you have excellent organisational skills and that you can cope with the demands and pressures of the job.

Sample question number 8

"Police officers must be capable of communicating effectively with lots of different people, both verbally and in writing. Please explain a situation when you had to tell an individual or group of people something that they may have found difficult or distressing. You will be assessed on how well you delivered the message and also on what you took into account when speaking to them."

PART 1 – Who were the people and what did you have to tell them?

"The people involved were my elderly next door neighbours. They had a cat that they had looked after for years and they were very fond of it. I had to inform them that their cat had just been run over by a car in the road."

PART 2 – Why do you think they may have found the message difficult or distressing?

"I was fully aware of how much they loved their cat and I could understand that the message I was about to tell them would have been deeply distressing. They had cherished the cat for years and to suddenly lose it would have been a great shock to them."

PART 3 – How did you deliver the message?

"To begin with I knocked at their door and asked calmly if I could come in to speak to them. Before I broke the news to them I made them a cup of tea and sat them down in a quiet room away from any distractions.

I then carefully and sensitively told them that their cat had passed away following an accident in the road. At all times I took into account their feelings and I made sure I delivered the message sensitively and in a caring manner."

PART 4 – Before you delivered your message, what did you take into account?

"I took into account where and when I was going to deliver the message. It was important to tell them in a quiet room away from any distractions so that they could grieve in peace. I also took into account the tone in which I delivered the message and I also made sure that I was sensitive to their feelings. I also made sure that I would be available to support them after I had broken the news."

- Read the question carefully and make sure that you answer every element of it. You may find on the application form that some of the questions are based around different core competencies. If this is the case then simply apply the same process of trying to match the core competencies by using keywords and phrases in your responses.

QUESTIONS BASED AROUND YOUR REASONS AND MOTIVATIONS FOR WANTING TO BECOME A POLICE OFFICER

In addition to the standard core competency based questions, you may be asked additional questions that are centred around your motivations for wanting to become a police officer with the PSNI. On the following pages, I have provided a number of different questions and sample responses to assist you. Please remember that the responses provided here, and in other parts of this guide, are for guidance purposes only. The responses you provide on your application form must be based around your own individual circumstances, beliefs and circumstances.

Sample question number 1

' How long have you been thinking about becoming a police officer and what has attracted you to the role?'

"I have been considering a career as a police officer ever since I started my current sales manager job approximately 7 years ago. I enjoy working in a customer focused environment and thrive on providing high levels of service to customers. I have always been aware that the role is demanding and highly challenging but the rewards of such a job far outweigh the difficulties. The opportunity to work as part of an efficient team and work towards providing the community with an effective service would be hugely satisfying."

- It is not advisable to state that you have only become interested recently. Candidates who have been seriously thinking about the job for a while will potentially score higher marks;

- In your response, try to demonstrate that you have studied the role carefully and that you believe your skills are suited to being a police officer;

- Candidates who state that they are attracted solely to the 'catching criminals' side of the role will not score highly;

- Read the core competencies and the job description carefully before responding to this question;

- Never be critical of a previous employer.

Sample question number 2

'What have you done to prepare for this application?'

"I have carried out a great deal of research to ascertain whether I am suitable for the role, and also to find out whether this career would suit my aspirations. I have intensively studied the police officer core competencies, to ensure that I can meet the expectations of the PSNI. I have also carried out extensive research prior to filling in my application form, instead of just applying and hoping to be successful. I spoke to several current serving officers at my local station, to ask them about the role and how it affects their day to day life. Finally, I have discussed my intentions with my immediate family, to ensure that I have their full support and encouragement."

- At the beginning of this guide, I placed great emphasis on how preparation leads to success. If you have carried out in-depth and meaningful preparation, and can demonstrate this, then you will massively boost your chances of success. This demonstrates to the force that you are serious about wanting the job.

FINAL TIPS FOR COMPLETING A SUCCESSFUL APPLICATION FORM

When filling out your form, your success will depend on your ability to do the following:

- Read the application form and the guidance notes at least twice before you complete it;

- If possible, photocopy the application form and complete a draft copy first. This will allow you to make any errors or mistakes without being penalised;

- Obtain a copy of the core competencies and have them at your side when completing the form;

- Take your time when completing the form, and set aside plenty of time for each question. I recommend that you spend five evenings completing the application form, breaking it down into manageable portions. This will allow you to maintain high levels of concentration;

- Complete the form in the correct ink colour. Your form could be thrown out for failing to follow simple instructions;

- Be honest when completing the form. If you are unsure about anything, contact the PSNI for confirmation;

- Try not to make any spelling or grammar errors. You WILL lose marks for poor spelling, grammar and punctuation;

- Try to use keywords and phrases which are relevant to the core competencies;

- Get someone to check over your form for errors before you submit it. If they can't read your application form, then the assessor probably won't be able to either;

- Take a photocopy of your final completed form before submitting it;

- Try to submit the form well before the closing date. The PSNI may operate a cut-off point in terms of the number of applications they receive;

- Some forms get lost in the post, so it is advisable that you send it by recorded delivery for peace of mind;

- If your form is unsuccessful, ask for feedback. It is important that you learn from your mistakes.

WHAT HAPPENS AFTER I HAVE SENT OFF MY APPLICATION FORM?

Once you have completed and sent off your application form, there will be a wait period before you find out whether or not you have been successful. If you are successful, you will be invited to take an Initial Selection Test (IST). This will be at a specified centre, at a particular time and date. In the next chapter, we will provide you with some sample questions from the test.

It is a good idea to prepare for the IST even before you receive your application result. By starting your preparation early, you will be giving yourself a 2-3 week advantage over other applicants; as 99% of applicants will wait to receive their result before they start to prepare.

CHAPTER 4

Initial Selection Test (IST)

The next stage of the application process is The Initial Selection Test. This is a series of exercises designed to filter out the weakest candidates to have made it through the application process. The PSNI receives thousands of applicants every year, and it would be impossible for them to put every candidate through to the assessment stage. Therefore, the IST is used as a pre-screening process.

The Initial Selection Test (IST) will consist of three sub tests, all of which will be held under timed conditions. The tests will examine the following skills:

• Your understanding of word meanings, logic and grammatical nuances;

• Your understanding and interpretation of language;

• Your understanding of verbal and numerical data.

It is important to prepare as comprehensively as you possibly can for the IST. Start preparing as early as possible, ideally this should be immediately after you have finished filling in the initial application form. The more preparation you do, the more confident you will feel, and this will reflect in your results. For many people, nerves can damage their chances of success, and therefore you need to do your utmost to reduce these nerves.

Some great ways to prepare for the IST are:

-**Read newspapers.** Using a pen and paper, read through an article and write down a list of definitive facts that have been established by the article. This will help you when it comes to the second part of the test. You could also try to spot any mistakes that have been missed by the editors. Alternatively, there are plenty of proof reading, spelling and grammar exercises you can find online.

-**Practice puzzles and crosswords.** These will help you to start thinking logically about puzzles and word problems.

-**Study data from tables, charts and graphs.** This is a really important exercise, as it will help you to see the way in which you should approach the actual numerical questions. This is the area where the majority of candidates struggle, and therefore it is essential that you are prepared to succeed where others fail.

Below we have included 3 sample tests, which will highlight the types of questions you can expect to answer. The majority of tests will require you to fill in your answers on a separate sheet of paper, allowing you to work quickly and efficiently.

READING COMPREHENSION

In this test you will be required to read through a passage, and identify a number of mistakes. These mistakes will be in the form of incorrect spelling, and words that have been used in the wrong context. You will be expected to read through the passage and underline the incorrect words. It is very important when taking this test that you:

- Underline the correct number of words as specified by the question, even if you can spot more mistakes;

- Underline only single words, not phrases or sentences;

- Only underline the words, do not try to correct them.

With this in mind, take a look at the example passage below. Identify eight mistakes in the passage, in under 3 minutes. We've provided the answers below, so you can identify any errors that you missed.

'Every Monday I pop round to my auntys house. She has recently remaried, and lives with her new husbond. There house is semi-detached, and contains all sorts of interesting ornaments. They live next door to a man who owns a german dog. The dog is always barking through the gate when I arrive, and I find it quite inmitidating. My aunty normally cooks me a hot dinner of sausage, beans and mash. This is one of my favourite meal, and therefore I always look foward to Monday evenings.'

ANSWERS TO READING COMPREHENSION:

1. 'auntys'

Explanation - The word 'auntys' should have an apostrophe before the s, to indicate that the house belongs to her.

2. 'remaried'

Explanation - The word 'remaried' should be spelt 'remarried'.

3. 'husbond'

Explanation - The word 'husbond' should be spelt 'husband'.

4. 'There'

Explanation - The word 'there' should be spelt 'their' since the house belongs to two or more people.

5. 'german'

Explanation-The word 'german' should be spelt with a capital letter, 'German'.

6. 'inmitidating'

Explanation - The word 'inmitidating' should be spelt 'intimidating'.

7. 'meal'

Explanation - The word 'meal' should be spelt 'meals'.

8. 'foward'

Explanation - The word 'foward' should be spelt 'forward'

VERBAL REASONING

In this test you will be given 4 separate passages, with a set number of statements after each. You will have to identify and then indicate on the answer sheet, whether you believe each statement to be **TRUE, FALSE** or **UNKNOWN**. The guidelines for each category are listed below:

TRUE: In order for a statement to qualify as true, the statement should be definitively made within the passage, or should be qualified by evidence taken from the passage that cannot be challenged.

FALSE: In order for a statement to qualify as false, the statement should be something that is not made in the passage, and should be something that can be challenged by reading the passage.

UNKNOWN: In order for a statement to qualify as unknown, there should be insufficient information in the passage to ascertain whether it is true or false.

In this test you should base your analysis on the assumption that everything stated in the passage is verbatim, and ignore any real world beliefs. Try to complete each question in 5 minutes or less. We have provided you with a number of different questions, rather than just two, to give you a better idea of how to go about answering this type of test.

Verbal Reasoning - Test 1

On the night of August 4th, a fire occurred in a nightclub belonging to Harry James. One person died in the fire, which happened at 11pm. The club was insured for less than its value. Harry James claims that he is devastated by the impact of the fire, which destroyed the entire building. Other buildings in the surrounding area, including Lolita's Pizza Bar, also incurred minor damages.

QUESTIONS – TRUE, FALSE OR UNKNOWN?

1. The fire occurred at 1100 hours.

True	False	Unknown

2. A relative of Harry James was killed in the fire.

True	False	Unknown

3. If the insurance company decide to pay out for the fire, Harry James stands to make a profit.

True	False	Unknown

4. The fire was caused by arson.

True	False	Unknown

5. The club was not insured at the time of the fire.

True	False	Unknown

Verbal Reasoning - Test 2

An accident occurred on the M6 motorway between junctions 8 and 9 southbound at 3pm. The driver of a Ford Fiesta was seen to pull into the middle lane without indicating, forcing another car to veer into the central reservation. One person suffered a broken arm and was taken to hospital before the police arrived.

QUESTIONS – TRUE, FALSE OR UNKNOWN?

1. The accident was on the M6 motorway on the carriageway that leads to Scotland.

True	False	Unknown

2. The driver of the Ford Fiesta was injured in the crash.

True	False	Unknown

3. The central reservation was responsible for the accident.

True	False	Unknown

4. The police did not give first aid at the scene.

True	False	Unknown

5. The accident happened at 1500 hours.

True	False	Unknown

Verbal Reasoning - Test 3

A man of between 30 and 35 years of age was seen stealing a car from outside Mrs Brown's house yesterday. He was seen breaking the nearside rear window with a hammer before driving off at 40 miles per hour. He narrowly missed a young mother who was pushing a pram. Mrs Brown is said to be inconsolable about the loss of her car, which she has had for many years before this incident. Police have called for more witnesses to come forward.

QUESTIONS – TRUE, FALSE OR UNKNOWN?

1. The man who stole the car was 34 years old.

True	False	Unknown

2. He stole Mrs Brown's car.

True	False	Unknown

3. The young mother who was pushing a pram was injured.

True	False	Unknown

4. He used a hammer to smash the windscreen.

True	False	Unknown

5. When he drove off he was breaking the speed limit.

True	False	Unknown

Verbal Reasoning - Test 4

A shopkeeper called Mr Smith was seen serving alcohol to a girl aged 16. The girl had shown him a fake ID, which was a driving licence belonging to her sister. The incident occurred at around 11.30pm on a Wednesday evening during December.

QUESTIONS – TRUE, FALSE OR UNKNOWN?

1. The girl is old enough to purchase alcohol from Mr Smith.

True	False	Unknown

2. The girl purchased the alcohol for her sister.

True	False	Unknown

3. The girl's sister had given the driving licence to her.

True	False	Unknown

4. Mr Smith will receive a custodial sentence for his actions.

True	False	Unknown

5. The girl was breaking the law.

True	False	Unknown

Answers to Verbal Reasoning Test 1 :

1. False

Explanation – The passage tells us that the fire occurred at 11pm, which in military time is 2300 hours.

2. Unknown

Explanation – While we are told that 1 person died, and Harry James is devastated, we have no way of knowing whether the person who died was related to him.

3. False

Explanation – The passage tells us that the club was insured for less than its value.

4. Unknown

Explanation – While we are told that there was a fire, we have no way of knowing whether it was arson or was caused by something else.

5. False

Explanation – We are told that the club was insured, but for less than its value.

Answers to Verbal Reasoning Test 2 :

1. False

Explanation – We are told that the accident happened on junctions 8 and 9 southbound. Scotland would be northbound.

2. Unknown

Explanation – We are not told any details about whether the driver of the Ford Fiesta was injured.

3. False

Explanation – The paragraph clearly indicates that the reason for the crash was that the driver of the Ford Fiesta pulled into the middle lane without indicating.

4. Unknown

Explanation – The paragraph stops before the police arrive, and therefore we have no details about what they did or didn't do.

5. True

Explanation – We are told that the accident occurred at 3pm, which is 1500 hours in military hours.

Answers to Verbal Reasoning Test 3:

1. Unknown

Explanation – We are only told that the man was between the ages of 30 and 35, not his exact age.

2. True

Explanation – We are told that Mrs Brown is inconsolable about the loss of her car.

3. False

Explanation – We are told that the car narrowly missed the mother and her pram.

4. False

Explanation – We are told that the man used a hammer to smash the rear view window.

5. Unknown

Explanation – We are told that the man drove off at 40mph, but we do not know if this is above the speed limit.

Answers to Verbal Reasoning Test 4:

1. False

Explanation – We are told that the girl is 16 years old, below the legal age to purchase alcohol.

2. Unknown

Explanation – We are not told anything about why the girl is purchasing alcohol.

3. Unknown

Explanation – We are told that the girl used her sister's driving license, but this does not mean that her sister gave it to her.

4. Unknown

Explanation – We are not told anything about what happened to Mr Smith as a result of selling alcohol to the girl.

5. True

Explanation – We know that the girl is below the legal age to purchase alcohol, therefore by doing so she was breaking the law.

DATA INTERPRETATION

In this test, you will be given a data sheet, and a series of questions based around the information contained within it. You will need to demonstrate your numerical ability and skills in data interpretation in order to find the correct answer.

The questions will all be multiple-choice, and could vary from larger more complex data sheets, to smaller more straightforward sheets.

We have provided you with two smaller sheets, to give you some idea of the types of questions you might expect to see:

Data Interpretation – Test 1

City Police have put out a tender for heating maintenance and installation. Below are quotes from 3 suppliers.

Heating, Maintenance and Installation	Supplier 1: Total cost over 3 years	Supplier 2: Total cost over 2 years	Supplier 3: Total cost over 5 years
Installation and boiler replacements	£24,630	£19,750	£36,150
Hot Air Systems	£142,530	£102,640	£229,850
Service and Maintenance	£17,880	£12,460	£25,625

1. Amongst all three suppliers, based on an annual cost, what is the average cost to install hot air systems?

A. £45,804

B. £50,000

C. £48,266

D. £47,655

Answer

2. Based on 2 years, what supplier provides the most expensive quote for installation and boiler replacements?

A. Supplier 1

B. Supplier 2

C. Supplier 3

D. Suppliers 1 and 3

Answer

3. What percentage of the total quote provided by Supplier 2 accounts for hot air systems?

A. 75%

B. 76.1%

C. 77.4%

D. 73.9%

Answer

Data Interpretation – Test 2

The Police Headquarters have put out a tender for fitness testing. Below are quotes from 3 suppliers.

Fitness Testing	Supplier 1: Total cost over 2 years	Supplier 2: Total cost over 3 years	Supplier 3: Total cost over 4 years
Basic Fitness Training	£9,800	£10,500	£16,650
Intense Fitness Training	£19,000	£23,500	£34,500
Eight week fitness programme	£16,000	£18,000	£33,000

1. What percentage of the total quote provided by Supplier 2 accounts for intense fitness training?

A. 43.5%

B. 45.2%

C. 46%

D. 44.9%

Answer

2. Based on an annual one year cost, which supplier provides the most expensive overall quote for basic fitness training?

A. Supplier 1

B. Supplier 2

C. Supplier 3

D. Supplier 1 and 3

Answer

3. Based on an annual one year cost, which supplier provides the cheapest 8 week Fitness programme?

A. Supplier 1

B. Supplier 2

C. Supplier 3

D. All the same

Answer

Answers to Data Interpretation Test 1:

1. *£48,266*

2. *Supplier 2*

3. *76.1%*

Answers to Data Interpretation Test 2:

1. *45.2%*

2. *Supplier 1*

3. *Supplier 1*

Hopefully the above exercises have given you a clearer idea about the three stages of the IST. To further aid you in your preparation, below we have included a mock test, which you should try to complete as efficiently as you can.

INITIAL SELECTION TEST-MOCK PAPER

Test 1:

Question 1

Read through the below passage and mark the errors by **underlining** the **words** that are wrong. You should identify **TEN** mistakes in the passage.

'Samuel Peters lives in Maidstone. He has a wif and too children. Every Sundays, Samuel takes his childran to see they're local team play football. The team plays at a parc that is just 5 minutes down the road from Samuels house. The team plays in a red and blue kit, and has the badge of a lion carrying a sword in it's mouth.

Samuel's son is a keen footballer, and often trains for his local district. In the furture, he hopes to play for a proffesional team.'

Question 2

Read through the below passage and mark the errors by **underlining** the **words** that are wrong. You should identify **TEN** mistakes in the passage.

'On Mondayz, Maria performs voluntarily work at her local library. She works from 9am till 4pm, and every other weak stays later until the evining. She spend's most of her time organising the book shelves, or worknig on the desk. Maria has become acustomed to dealing with the libraries' regular service users, and particulrly enjoys helping people to find books'.

Question 3

Read through the below passage and mark the errors by **underlining** the **words** that are wrong. You should identify **TEN** mistakes in the passage.

'The Ficshire Sailing Sociaty play an importent role in the local community. When not sailing, the members of the sociaty can oftan be seen performing comunity based task's, such as litter patrolz and memorial painting. Due to they're outstanding behaviour, the local authority recently awardad them with a medal for excelence.'

Question 4

Read through the below passage and mark the errors by **underlining** the **words** that are wrong. You should identify **TEN** mistakes in the passage.

'Climate change is a result of human actian. Over the past 15 decades, the world has become more industriailised, and this has changed the balonce of the carbon cylce. Burning fossil fuel's is a clear example of this. This releaeses carbon dixide into the atmosphere, and causes higher global tempatures and risez in sea level's.'

Question 5

Read through the below passage and mark the errors by **underlining** the **words** that are wrong. You should identify **TEN** mistakes in the passage.

'Recent technlogical changes have imposed upon the world of television. Where televizion continus to use markating strategies that are several year's old, the internet is develping at a rapid pace. It has been subject to dynamik changes, particulrly in advertising and marketing. Soon, televizion will be left behinde.'

Question 6

Read through the below passage and mark the errors by **underlining** the **words** that are wrong. You should identify **TEN** mistakes in the passage.

'The use of artificiel enhancments and banned substances in sport is commonly known as 'doping'. These substance's illegally help the user to gain an advantage over there competition. The act of doping fundmentally diminshes the spirit of sport and what it represents. Dopers damage the reputatation of sport in society, and make it difficult to mantain an image of sport as truthful, cleane and faire.'

Question 7

Read through the below passage and mark the errors by **underlining** the **words** that are wrong. You should identify **TEN** mistakes in the passage.

'Work experience gained during universty year's, can be hugly advantageos to graduate's looking for employment. Employer's are no longer basing their choices on education qualifications, or on the best scores. Incentivez from highr authorites have become increasingly focused on internships and work expeirience placements. This is great for graduates who wish to obtain a better job after their universty years.'

Question 8

Read through the below passage and mark the errors by **underlining** the **words** that are wrong. You should identify **TEN** mistakes in the passage.

'In order to aid Third Word countires, tourism needs to enngage with the promotion of growth and development in not only the rural areas of countries, but also with women, youth and the enviroment. Mass tourism has been blamd for exploting poorer countries, and

endangering biodivesity. Tourism is frequently blamed for usin up these countries limited resrouces, in an inefficient and wastful manner.'

Question 9

Read through the below passage and mark the errors by **underlining** the **words** that are wrong. You should identify **TEN** mistakes in the passage.

'Critics are urging teachers at all levelz of educaton to equip students with the right skils and knowledge to be able to sift through and interpret information found online, and assess its plausibiility. The youth of todaiy have become so obssessed with the internet, that they struggle to differentiaite between anecdotial and unsubstatianted material that is posted onlin.'

Question 10

Read through the below passage and mark the errors by **underlining** the **words** that are wrong. You should identify **TEN** mistakes in the passage.

'Researche indictes that people who take supplemments for Vitamin C of over 5000 milligrams per day, arre more at risck of developing cancar. Health suplemments, despite the constent advertising of health benefits, are shown too be causing both short-term and long-term healh issue's.'

Test 2:

Read through the passages, and then identify whether the statements that follow are TRUE, FALSE or UNKNOWN.

Question 1

Following a bank robbery in the town centre, 6 masked gunmen were seen speeding away from the scene in a black van. The incident, which happened in broad daylight in front of hundreds of shoppers, was picked up by CCTV footage. Police are appealing for witnesses. The local newspaper has offered a £5,000 reward for any information leading to the conviction of all the people involved.

QUESTIONS – TRUE, FALSE OR UNKNOWN?

1. The gunmen drove off in black van.

True	False	Unknown

2. Someone must have seen something.

True	False	Unknown

3. The incident was picked up by CCTV cameras.

True	False	Unknown

4. The newspaper will pay £5,000 for information leading to the arrest of all of the men involved.

True	False	Unknown

5. Police are not appealing to members of the public for help.

True	False	Unknown

Question 2

A factory fire at 'Stevenage Supplies' was arson, the police have confirmed. A man was seen running away from the scene shortly before the fire started. Earlier that day a man was sacked from the company for allegedly stealing money from the safe. The incident is the second one to occur at the factory in as many months.

QUESTIONS – TRUE, FALSE OR UNKNOWN?

1. Police have confirmed that the fire at the factory was arson.

True	False	Unknown

2. The man who was seen running away from the fire was the man who started it.

True	False	Unknown

3. One previous 'fire-related' incident has already occurred at the factory.

True	False	Unknown

4. The man who was sacked from the factory may have started the fire.

True	False	Unknown

5. The incident is the second fire to occur this month.

True	False	Unknown

Question 3

At 1800 hours today police issued a statement in relation to the crime scene at Armstrong Road. Police have been examining the scene all day and reports suggest that it may be murder. Forensic officers have been visiting the incident and inform us that the whole street has been cordoned off and nobody will be allowed through. Police say that the street involved will be closed for another 18 hours and no access will be available to anyone during this time.

QUESTIONS – TRUE, FALSE OR UNKNOWN?

1. Police have confirmed the incident is murder.

True	False	Unknown

2. Forensic officers have now left the scene.

True	False	Unknown

3. The road will be open at 12 noon the following day.

True	False	Unknown

4. Although the street has been cordoned off, taxis and buses will be given access.

True	False	Unknown

5. Forensic officers will be at the scene all night.

True	False	Unknown

Question 4

Mrs Rogers telephoned the police at 8pm to report a burglary at her house in Gamble Crescent. She reports that she came home from work and her front bedroom window was open but she doesn't remember leaving it open. She informs the police that her jewellery box is missing and also £40 cash, which was left on the kitchen table. She came home from work at 5pm and left again at 7am in the morning. No other signs of forced entry were visible.

QUESTIONS – TRUE, FALSE OR UNKNOWN?

1. The burglar made his/her way in through the bedroom window.

True	False	Unknown

2. The burglar took the jewellery and £40 cash before leaving.

True	False	Unknown

3. Mrs Rogers was away from the house for 10 hours in total.

True	False	Unknown

4. Mrs Rogers may have left the window open herself before leaving for work.

True	False	Unknown

5. There were other visible signs of forced entry.

True	False	Unknown

Question 5

The smoking ban was brought in to the UK to stop people from smoking in public places i.e. restaurants, pubs, workplaces etc. Martin believes that this legislation that has been implemented is a breach of his human rights and privacy. Martin was given an £80 fine for smoking on three different occasions in the space of a one month period.

QUESTIONS-TRUE, FALSE OR UNKNOWN?

1. Martin believes that the smoking ban is a breach of his human rights.

True	False	Unknown

2. There was at least one week during the month when Martin did not get fined for smoking in a public place.

True	False	Unknown

3. Martin believes the right to privacy and being able to smoke where and when you want is more important than the health of other people whom he is smoking around.

True	False	Unknown

4. The smoking ban was brought in to reduce the number of people being diagnosed with cancer.

True	False	Unknown

5. Martin was fined £240 in total.

True	False	Unknown

Question 6

A parent went into a school and demanded a meeting with the headmaster. She complained about the lack of action regarding anti-social behaviour. She claimed that her son was being bullied when a boy in the year above pulled his seat out from beneath him. The headmaster emphasised the importance of distinguishing between behaviour that is typical 'boy banter', harmless fun and behaviour that was inappropriate and victimising.

QUESTIONS-TRUE, FALSE OR UNKNOWN?

1. The headmaster did not classify the behaviour of pulling out the child's seat from beneath him as bullying.

True	False	Unknown

2. The headmaster was the person who pulled the boy's chair out from beneath him.

True	False	Unknown

3. The boy being accused of bullying was older than the boy whose chair he pulled out.

True	False	Unknown

4. The headmaster does not have an issue with 'typical boy banter'.

True	False	Unknown

5. The meeting between the headmaster and the boy's Mother took place at the school.

True	False	Unknown

Question 7

A woman has recently given birth to twins – a boy and a girl. During her first week home she sets them into a routine. She knows that around 5pm, her son begins to cry because it is his feeding time. Her daughter wakes up a little later. The woman has not seen her husband for several days.

QUESTIONS-TRUE, FALSE OR UNKNOWN?

1. The woman gave birth to twins last week.

True	False	Unknown

2. The woman's husband has left her to raise the children alone.

True	False	Unknown

3. The woman's daughter wakes up at 3pm every day.

True	False	Unknown

4. The woman's son cries because he is hungry.

True	False	Unknown

5. The woman's husband had an affair.

True	False	Unknown

Question 8

A bank was robbed on Saturday afternoon. The incident happened at 4pm, and both the police and paramedics arrived at 20 past 4. They immediately began treating victims and arresting people. There were 8 hostages, 3 of them employees at the bank. A man in a balaclava pointed a gun at one of the bankers and demanded the money from her till. She handed the money to the man in the balaclava, at the same time as he was tackled from behind by one of the hostages. A gunshot went off.

QUESTIONS-TRUE, FALSE OR UNKNOWN?

1. The banker who handed over the money was a man.

True	False	Unknown

2. The man in the balaclava escaped with the money from the till.

True	False	Unknown

3. The man who tackled the robber from behind was shot.

True	False	Unknown

4. The robbery had finished by 20 past 4.

True	False	Unknown

5. 5 of the hostages were customers at the bank.

True	False	Unknown

Question 9

On Tuesday, a hundred students attended the National Gallery in London. The Gallery has over 2,300 masterpieces, which range from contemporary art to late medieval sculptures. It is believed that 1 of these students stole a valuable vase from the medieval exhibition. CCTV footage caught an individual wearing a hood sneaking out from one of the unmanned, back entrances. The individual had long, blonde hair, but their face was not distinguishable. Since the incident, security measures have been stepped up. Police are urging witnesses to come forward, and the guard in charge of manning the exhibit has apologised profusely for the incident.

QUESTIONS-TRUE, FALSE OR UNKNOWN?

1. A girl stole the vase.

True	False	Unknown

2. The person who stole the vase has not yet been caught.

True	False	Unknown

3. The person in the hood stole the vase.

True	False	Unknown

4. There were no security measures in place to prevent the vase from being stolen.

True	False	Unknown

5. The guard has been fired.

True	False	Unknown

Question 10

At 11am on Wednesday morning, the police were called to an incident. A middle aged male was found shot dead on the upper floor of a housing development project. Another construction worker was also found dead. The only witness to the crime was the building development manager, who claims his life was spared to send a message. He said that there were two shooters, both with masks over their faces. One of the shooters wore a bow tie.

QUESTIONS-TRUE, FALSE OR UNKNOWN?

1. The shooters shot the construction worker.

True	False	Unknown

2. The shooting occurred at 1100 hours.

True	False	Unknown

3. The shooters were male.

True	False	Unknown

4. The building development manager could not identify the shooters.

True	False	Unknown

5. The middle aged male was killed with a shotgun.

True	False	Unknown

Test 3:

Look through the data sheets and answer the questions below.

Ficshire Police have put out a tender for uniform dry cleaning and alterations. Below are quotes from 3 suppliers:

Uniform dry cleaning and amendments	Supplier 1: Total cost over 1 years	Supplier 2: Total cost over 3 years	Supplier 3: Total cost over 2 years
Dry Cleaning	£9,600	£26,700	£19,020
Alterations	£5,500	£14,900	£11,000
Cleaning and alterations-full package	£13,450	£38,850	£25,800

1. Based on an annual one year cost, which supplier provides the cheapest dry cleaning services?

A. Supplier 1

B. Supplier 2

C. Supplier 3

D. All the same

Answer

2. For the total cost over 3 years, what supplier provides the cheapest quote overall for cleaning and alterations– full package?

A. Supplier 1

B. Supplier 2

C. Supplier 3

D. All the same

Answer

3. Based on their annual cost and everything that the supplier has to offer, what supplier is the most expensive?

A. Supplier 1

B. Supplier 2

C. Supplier 3

D. All the same

Answer

Ficshire Police have put out a tender for electrical equipment and supplies. Below are quotes from 3 suppliers:

Electrical Equipment and Supplies	Supplier 1: Total cost over 2 years	Supplier 2: Total cost over 2 years	Supplier 3: Total cost over 1 year
Basic Services	£34,550	£36,660	£15,450
Electrical Safety Test	£39,550	£42,000	£20,000
Full equipment maintenance	£120,850	£150,500	£60,000

4. Based on an annual year cost, which supplier offers the best price for electrical safety checks?

A. Supplier 1

B. Supplier 2

C. Supplier 3

D. They are the same

Answer

5. What percentage of the total quote provided by supplier 1 accounts for basic services?

A. 17%

B. 17.7%

C. 18.5%

D. 18.3%

Answer

6. Based on 2 years, what supplier provides the cheapest quote overall for electrical equipment and supplies?

A. Supplier 1

B. Supplier 2

C. Supplier 3

D. Supplier 2 and 3

Answer

The table below shows the sales across 6 countries for the model BMW for a 6 month period. The BMW's are imported to each country from a main dealer:

Country	Jan	Feb	Mar	April	May	June	Total
UK	21	28	15	35	31	20	150
Germany	45	48	52	36	41	40	262
France	32	36	33	28	20	31	180
Brazil	42	41	37	32	35	28	215
Spain	22	26	17	30	24	22	141
Italy	33	35	38	28	29	38	201
Total	195	214	192	189	180	179	1149

7. What percentage of the overall total was sold in April?

A. 17.8%

B. 17.2%

C. 18.9%

D. 16.4%

E. 21.6%

Answer

8. What percentage of the overall total sales were sold to the French importers?

A. 15.7%

B. 18.2%

C. 18.9%

D. 25.6%

E. 24.5%

Answer

9. What percentage of the total imports is accounted for by the two smallest importers?

A. 35.6%

B. 25.3%

C. 22.6%

D. 28.1%

E. 29.1%

Answer

The table below shows the sales across 6 European countries for the NSR500 Motorcycle for a 6 month period. The NSR500 Motorcycle is imported to each country from a main dealer.

Country	Jan	Feb	Mar	April	May	June	Total
UK	32	36	28	21	42	46	205
Germany	42	51	53	49	41	35	271
France	12	18	21	15	28	21	115
Belgium	16	18	19	22	21	25	121
Spain	35	31	26	27	31	35	185
Italy	35	38	41	28	36	42	220
Total	172	192	188	162	199	204	1117

10. What is the average number of units per month imported to Germany over the 6 month period?

A. 35.6%

B. 45.2%

C. 52.4%

D. 54.6%

E. 31.8 %

Answer

11. What percentage of total imports is accounted for by the three smallest importers?

A. 27.8%

B. 31.7%

C. 37.7%

D. 42.7%

E. 37.1%

Answer

12. What is the difference between the average number of units per month imported by Spain over the first 4 months, and the average number of units per month imported by the UK over the first 4 months?

A. 0.5

B. 1.5

C. 2

D. 4

E. 5.5

Answer

The below table shows the number of divorces across 6 different countries for a 6 month period.

Country	Jan	Feb	Mar	April	May	June	Total
UK	356	258	129	352	312	258	1665
Germany	357	325	259	257	329	316	1843
France	201	285	210	285	236	196	1413
Belgium	95	85	109	83	91	108	571
Spain	148	156	201	122	189	175	991
Italy	138	254	169	147	168	96	972
Total	1295	1363	1077	1246	1325	1149	7455

13. What is the average number of divorces per month in Spain

over the first 5 months of the year?

A. 158.3
B. 162.5
C. 163.2
D. 163.9
E. 161.8

Answer

14. What percentage of total divorces is accounted for by the three lowest divorce rate countries?

A. 34%
B. 31%
C. 28%
D. 35%
E. 41%

Answer

15. What is the average number of divorces per month for Germany over the 6 month period?

A. 301.5
B. 303.6
C. 300
D. 306.2
E. 307.2

Answer

The below table shows the number of births in the south east, UK, in a 12 month period. The table shows data from the years 2008-2013.

Year	Jan-Feb	Mar-April	May-Jun	Juy-Aug	Sept-Oct	Nov-Dec	Total
2008	352	302	254	216	169	320	1613
2009	310	296	242	241	190	313	1592
2010	286	273	249	214	168	146	1336
2011	234	216	206	165	172	210	1203
2012	196	176	135	167	166	106	946
2013	118	123	185	135	147	109	817
Total	1496	1386	1271	1138	1012	1204	7507

16. What is the difference between the year that had the lowest number of births and the year that had the highest number of births?

A. 721

B. 712

C. 796

D. 769

E. 779

Answer

17. What percentage of the total number of births is accounted for by the three years that have the highest number of births?

A. 75%

B. 72.5%

C. 61.5%

D. 60.5%

E. 55.5%

Answer

18. What percentage of the overall total was the birth rate between Nov-Dec?

A. 12%

B. 14%

C. 16%

D. 18%

E. 20%

Answer

The below table shows the sales across 6 European countries for the Jaguar XK car for a 6 month period. The Jaguar XK is imported to each country from a main dealer.

Country	Jan	Feb	Mar	April	May	June	Total
UK	115	85	72	93	116	135	616
Germany	285	214	206	185	147	163	1200
France	86	74	67	101	62	71	461
Belgium	48	46	59	93	82	103	431
Spain	108	139	195	146	127	101	816
Italy	215	189	165	147	256	210	1182
Total	857	747	764	765	790	783	4706

19. What is average number of units per month imported to Spain over the 6 month period?

A. 163

B. 136

C. 140

D. 146

E. 121

Answer

20. What percentage of total imports is accounted for by the three smallest importers?

A. 32%

B. 12%

C. 52%

D. 22%

E. 17%

Answer

21. What is the difference between the average number of units per month imported by Germany over the first 4 months, and the average number of units per month imported by the UK over the first 4 months?

A. 180.75

B. 180.25

C. 131.75

D. 150

E. 131.25

Answer

The below table shows the number of people unemployed in the south east, UK, following a 12 month period. The table shows data from the years 2008 – 2013.

Year	Jan-Feb	Mar-April	May-Jun	July-Aug	Sept-Oct	Nov-Dec	Total
2008	89	106	111	113	125	164	708
2009	92	93	123	127	148	152	735
2010	109	159	176	130	169	162	905
2011	201	194	157	165	138	139	994
2012	253	249	239	258	247	219	1465
2013	213	139	219	243	216	206	1236
Total	957	940	1025	1036	1043	1042	6043

22. What was the average number of people unemployed in the 12 month period of 2010?

A. 75.4

B. 82.2

C. 71.4

D. 80

E. 65.5

Answer

23. What is the mean number of unemployed people between July and August?

A. 156.5

B. 152.7

C. 172.7

D. 182.6

E. 168.2

Answer

24. What percentage of the overall total was the unemployment rate between Nov-Dec?

A. 21.2%

B. 28.2%

C. 17.2%

D. 32.2%

E. 40.2%

Answer

ANSWERS TO MOCK TEST

Test 1:

1. The words underlined should be: **wif, too, Sundays, childran, they're, parc, Samuels, it's, furture, proffesional.**

2. The words underlined should be: **Mondayz, voluntarily, weak, evining, spend's, worknig, acustomed, libraries', particulrly, books'.**

3. The words underlined should be: **Sociaty, importent, sociaty, oftan, comunity, task's, patrolz, they're, awardad, excelence.**

4. The words underlined should be: **actian, industriailised, balonce, cylce, fuel's, releaeses, dixide, tempatures, risez, level's.**

5. The words underlined should be: **technlogical, televizion, continus, markating, year's, develping, dynamik, particulrly, televizion, behinde.**

6. The words underlined should be: **artificiel, enhancments, substance's, there, fundmentally, diminshes, reputatation, maintain, cleane, faire.**

7. The words underlined should be: **year's, hugly, advantageos, graduate's, employer's, incentivez, highr, authorites, expeirience, universty.**

8. The words underlined should be: **word, countires, enngage, enviroment, blamd, exploting, biodivesity, usin, resorces, wastful.**

9. The words underlined should be: **levelz, educaton, skils, plausibiility, todaiy, obssesed, differentiaite, anecdotial, unsubstantianted, onlin.**

10. The words underlined should be: **Researche, indictes, supplemments, arre, risck, cancar, suplememnts, constent, too, healh.**

Test 2:

Question 1.

1. True
2. Unknown
3. True
4. False
5. False

Question 2:

1. True
2. Unknown
3. True
4. True
5. True

Question 3:

1. False
2. Unknown
3. True
4. False
5. Unknown

Question 4:

1. Unknown
2. Unknown
3. False
4. True
5. False

Question 5:

1. True

2. True

3. Unknown

4. Unknown

5. False

Question 6:

1. Unknown

2. False

3. True

4. Unknown

5. True

Question 7:

1. True

2. Unknown

3. False

4. True

5. Unknown

Question 8:

1. False

2. Unknown

3. Unknown

4. True

5. Unknown

Question 9:

1. Unknown
2. True
3. Unknown
4. False
5. Unknown

Question 10:

1. Unknown
2. False
3. Unknown
4. True
5. Unknown

<u>Test 3:</u>

Question 1

1. Supplier 2
2. Supplier 3
3. Supplier 1

Question 2

4. Supplier 1
5. 17.7%
6. Supplier 3

Question 3

7. D = 16.4%
8. A = 15.7%
9. B = 25.3%

Question 4

10. B = 45.2
11. C = 37.7%
12. A = 0.5

Question 5

13. C = 163.2
14. A = 34%
15. E = 307.2

Question 6

16. C = 796
17. D = 60.5%
18. A = 12%

Question 7

19. B = 136
20. A = 32%
21. E = 131.25

Question 8

22. A = 75.4
23. B = 152.7
24. C = 17.2%

IST PREPARATION TIPS

Before the test:

- Make sure you get a good night's sleep;

- Allow yourself lots of time to locate and travel to the assessment centre.

During the test:

- Listen to, and read, all of the instructions extremely carefully;

- Don't be afraid to ask questions if you are unsure about something;

- Make sure you read each question thoroughly before answering;

- Work as quickly and accurately as you possibly can;

- Don't waste time answering questions that you are stuck on. Move on and come back to them at the end if you have time.

If you are successful in your endeavours, you will be invited to attend an assessment centre, which will further examine your skills. In the next chapter, we will provide you with all of the information you need to know about the assessment centre, the exercises you'll have to perform, and the type of preparation you should do.

CHAPTER 5

Assessment Centre

Once you have successfully passed the Initial Selection Test (IST), you will be invited to attend an assessment centre. Make sure that once you are provided with details, times and location, you work out exactly where the location is, in order to ensure that you do not arrive late. The assessment centre is designed to assess your suitability for recruitment into the PSNI. It is usually conducted over a period of five hours, and you will be required to bring a number of important documents with you in order to confirm your identification to the police.

You will need to bring:

• A valid passport;

• A driving license;

• A birth certificate, issued within six weeks of birth;

• A cheque book and bank card with three statements and a proof of signature;

• Proof of residence; e.g. council tax, gas, electricity, water or telephone bill.

Make sure that you read all of the information that is given to you, and take along the relevant documents. If you do not, then you won't be able to take part in the day. Finally, you'll need to prepare 100% beforehand, in order to ensure you are ready for the challenges you will face.

How to prepare for the assessment centre:

From preparing for the application form and IST, you will have already learnt a considerable amount of job specific information that is relevant to the role of a police officer. Once again, the core competencies will form the basis of your preparation, and you should have a copy of them next to you when preparing for each stage of the assessment centre.

There are three stages to the assessment centre. These include:

- Three role-play exercises;

- A written exercise;

- An interview.

In relation to the written tests, only you will know your current skill level, and the amount of time necessary to prepare yourself fully for this area. Within the next two chapters, you will receive some invaluable advice relating to every area of the assessment, so make sure that you read it carefully and try out the sample test questions. While the role-play exercises can be a really daunting experience; if you practice beforehand, then your confidence will increase dramatically. We have provided you with thorough and detailed explanations on how to prepare for each area, and the best way to answer the questions. Always remember to centre your role-play preparation around the core competencies, as this is how you will be assessed.

THE ROLE-PLAY/INTERACTIVE EXERCISES

During the PSNI assessment centre, you will have to partake in three role-play exercises. The type of situation that you will be confronted with varies greatly. However, examples of the type of exercises which have been used in the past include:

- A customer of a shopping centre, who wants to discuss an incident that happened at the centre;

- A shop owner in the centre, who wants to discuss an incident that happened in their shop;

- An employee of the centre, who has been asked to attend a meeting.

The situation that you will have to deal with is largely irrelevant. What matters is the way that you interact with the role-play actor, and that you say the right things to ensure you score highly on your assessment. You must be able to demonstrate the police officer core competencies during each role-play scenario.

In order to show strong levels of proficiency and professionalism within your role-play exercises, make sure you consider the following areas:

- Make sure that you deal with the role-play actor in a sensitive and supportive manner;

- Demonstrate respect for other people's views and feelings;

- Show that you can see issues from other people's point of view;

- Ask relevant questions to clarify the situation;

- Listen to people's needs and interests;

- Respect confidentiality where appropriate;

- Present an appropriate image;

- Try to sort out customer issues as efficiently as possible;

- Make reference to supporting documentation, policies and procedures;

- Ensure that the customer is happy with the solution that you have provided;

- Keep the customer updated on any progress that you have made.

It is crucial that you learn the core competencies, and that you are able to demonstrate them during each exercise. This part of the selection process will be split into two, five minute parts. The first part will consist of the preparation phase, and the second part will be the actual role-play exercise.

'Preparation phase'

Prior to the actual role-play, you will be given a card or piece of paper that provides you with information on the scenario in which you will be tested. This is known as the *'preparation phase'*. You may also be provided with additional documentation that is relevant to the scenario that you'll be required to deal with. You will be taken to a desk or a separate room, where you will have just five minutes to prepare and take notes, which can be used during the second phase. You need to make maximum use of your notes, as you will not be permitted to use any writing utensils during the next phase. At the end of the 'activity' phase, you will be required to hand in your notes to the assessor.

As someone who has been through this type of role-play assessment, I found that learning the welcome pack prior to the assessment day made the task a lot easier. The preparation phase was easy, simply because I knew the role of a customer service officer inside out. I knew the code of conduct, the equality policy statement, and all of the other information that was applicable to the role. As soon as I turned over the card that told me what my scenario would be about, I knew exactly what I was required to do.

<u>You need to make sure that you use your preparation time wisely. Here is how I would recommend that you do it:</u>

• Quickly read the scenario and any supporting information/ documentation. If you have already studied the welcome pack prior to your assessment, breaking down this information will be much easier;

- Once you have studied the scenario, and any additional information/documentation, you should then try to separate all of the relevant information from the irrelevant information. Highlight and take brief notes on what you think is the most relevant;

- You now need to cross reference any relevant information from the scenario with procedures, policies and responsibilities that are listed in the welcome pack. For example, if within the scenario it becomes apparent that someone is being bullied, you will need to use and make reference to the equality policy statement. Another example could be if a child has been reported missing, in which case, you would need to make use of security guards, the tannoy system and the CCTV cameras that are posted around the centre;

- Finally, I would recommend that you write down a step-by-step approach as to how you intend to deal with the customer. An example of this could be as follows:

STEP 1:

- Introduce yourself to the role actor and ask him/her how you can help them. Remember to be polite and respectful and treat the role-play actor in a sensitive and supportive manner. You are being assessed against the core competency of respect for race and diversity during every role-play scenario;

STEP 2:

- Listen to the actor carefully and ask them relevant questions in order to establish the facts. For example: *how, when, where, why and who;*

STEP 3:

- Clarify the information received, in order to check that you have understood the situation as clearly as possible;

STEP 4:

- Provide a suitable solution to the problem or situation, and inform the role-play actor of what you intend to do. Remember to use keywords and phrases from the core competencies;

STEP 5:

- Check to confirm that the role-play actor is happy with your solution. Provide a final summary of what you intend to do, and ask them if there is anything else that you can help them with. Tell them that you will take responsibility for solving the problem, and will keep them updated on the progress of the situation.

Once you have made your notes and created a plan of action, you are now ready to go through to the activity phase. Below I have provided you with an actual demonstration of how you might want to approach the preparation phase, using a sample scenario.

SAMPLE ROLE-PLAY EXERCISE 1 = 'PREPARATION' PHASE

You are the customer service manager at a retail centre. A member of your staff approaches you and tells you that she has been bullied by another member of staff. The woman is clearly upset by the situation and she wants you to take action.

How to prepare

If you have already taken the time to study your 'Welcome Pack' prior to the assessment, then the first thing that will spring to mind is the equality policy statement. Within this statement, you will find specific details about how to deal with situations of this nature. It is essential that you follow each step carefully. Below I've shown you how I would use my 5 step plan to deal with this scenario in an effective and professional manner.

STEP 1:

I would walk into the activity room and introduce myself to the role actor. I would ask them sensitively what the problem was and how I could help them. If there was a chair available in the room, then I would ask them to sit down.

STEP 2:

I would listen very carefully to what they have to say and sympathise where appropriate. I would then start to establish the facts of the case, by asking them the following types of questions:

- How long has the bullying been going on for?

- Who was involved and what were they doing/saying?

- Were there any other people involved?

- Have there been any witnesses to the incident?

- Have you asked them to stop their behaviour, and what was their reaction?

STEP 3:

I would clarify and confirm with the role actor that I had gathered all of the correct facts and information.

STEP 4:

At this stage I would take full control of the situation and tell the role actor what I intended to do about the situation. I would make reference to the equality policy statement, and would use this as a basis for solving the problem. I would also make use of keywords and phrases that matched the 'core competencies' of the situation (ultimately bettering your chances of a successful response).

STEP 5:

During the final stages of the role-play, I would check to confirm that the role-play actor is happy with my intended solution. I would provide them with a final summary of my intentions, and I would ask if there was anything else that I can help them with. At this stage, I would also confirm to them that I was going to take responsibility for resolving their problem, and agree to keep them updated on progress as and when it occurred.

Once the 5 minute preparation phase is complete, a buzzer will sound, and you will move onto the activity stage of the assessment.

'The Activity Phase'

The activity stage will again last for 5 minutes, and it is during this phase that you are required to interact with the role actor. During the activity stage, there will be an assessor in the room, whose responsibility is to assess you against the core competencies. Try to ignore them and concentrate fully on how you interact with the actor. There may also be a third person in the room, who will be there to shadow the assessor. You'll be assessed on what you did, and how well you did it. You will normally receive a grade from A-D, with A being the highest. While you should always aim for an A, don't be too disheartened if you feel that you haven't done well on a particular exercise, as you can always make up your grades in another.

*Please note, if you score a D against the core competency of respect for race and diversity, then you will **fail** the entire assessment.*

During the previous sample role-play exercise, we focused on a complaint made by a member of staff who claimed that she was being bullied by another member of the team. Within the equality policy statement, you will find suggested courses of action. The options here may suggest that person asks the offender to stop, that the problem is discussed with an appropriate person, or to make a formal complaint.

Below I have provided you with some suggested responses to this type of exercise, followed by an explanation. While most of these can be applied to similar exercises surrounding harassment, you should try to judge every situation separately and act according to the brief.

Sample responses and actions to exercise 1:

You are the customer service manager at a retail centre. A member of your staff approaches you and tells you that she has been bullied by another member of staff. The woman is clearly upset by the situation and she wants you to take action.

Response 1

"Thank you for coming to see me today. I understand that you have a problem with another member of staff?"

Explanation:

In this response, you are demonstrating a level of customer care and awareness, and ultimately show a clear focus in regards to the needs of the individual. Remember to use open body language and never come across as confrontational, defensive or aggressive.

Response 2

"Would you be able to tell me exactly what has happened and how this has affected you? I will also need to ask you who was involved, where it has been occurring, and on how many occasions it has happened? Please try to include dates and times."

Explanation:

Again you are focusing on the needs of the individual, which is imperative to the role of being a police officer. Try to look and sound genuine and also use suitable facial expressions. In order to 'solve the issue', you must first ask questions and gather the facts about the incident.

Response 3

"It must have been very difficult for you to bring this matter to my attention, I appreciate you coming to see me."

Explanation:

During this response you are demonstrating a caring nature and you are providing a high level of service.

Response 4

"Have you asked them to stop or informed anybody else of this situation? Are you aware of this happening to anyone else?"

Explanation:

Here you are gathering the facts, which will help you to provide a suitable resolution to the problem.

Response 5

"The company equality policy in relation to this kind of alleged behaviour is quite clear, it states XYZ. It will NOT be tolerated and I can assure you the matter will be dealt with."

Explanation:

During this response, you are detailing the company equality policy. This demonstrates to the assessor that you not only are fully aware of the policies and procedures, but you are also showing your knowledge to determine behaviour that is unacceptable. This demonstrates not only your ability to analyse a particular situation, but also highlights the 'core competencies' on which you are being assessed.

Response 6

"Before I detail my solution to this problem, I want to confirm all of the details of the case. Please can you confirm that..."

Explanation:

During this response you are confirming and checking that the details that you have obtained are correct. This is a crucial stage as it demonstrates your ability to recall large amounts of information given to you in a short space of time; a duty that is common to the role of a police officer.

Response 7

"Please be aware that you can make a formal complaint if you wish to do so. Your feelings and wishes are paramount during my investigation. What would you like to happen from here? Would you like to make a formal complaint against the individual concerned, or deal with the situation in an alternative way?"

Explanation:

By asking the person what they want to do, you are demonstrating an ability to put their needs first, and giving them the choice as to how the situation should be dealt with. You need to remain objective, and not persuade them in any way.

Response 8

"Let me assure you that this matter will be dealt with as a priority, but in the meantime I will place another member of staff with you so that you can work in a comfortable environment. Are you happy with this course of action?"

Explanation:

Here you are taking action to resolve the problem. You are also informing the person of how you intend to resolve the situation for the time being. Finally, you are checking that the person is satisfied with the course of action that is going to be taken.

Response 9

"May I thank you again for bringing this matter to my attention. I assure you that I will keep you fully informed of all progress. I wish to inform you that I will be taking personal responsibility for resolving this issue. Is there anything else I can do for you?"

Explanation:

Finally, you are demonstrating a high level of service and also checking if there is anything else that you can do for them. You are also taking personal responsibility for resolving the issue. It is important to tell them that you will keep them informed of the outcome of any investigation.

Sample role-play exercise 2

You are the customer service officer at a retail centre. A school teacher has lost a pupil in the shopping centre and he wants to discuss the matter with you. He is very annoyed that it took him so long to find your office. He states that there were no security staff around and his pupil has now been missing for fifteen minutes. He wants to know what you intend to do about it.

How to prepare and possible actions to consider:

- To begin with, you should study the 'OPERATIONS' information about the centre. What does it say that possibly relate to the above scenario? Is there any CCTV?

- Are there any security staff that could help look for any missing persons?

- Is there a police station within the complex and can the police be used to respond to situations like this?

- Request the attendance of the police immediately;

- Make sure that you keep the teacher in the office with you so that they can provide further information to the police about the missing child;

- Try to gather information about the missing child – How old are they? What are they wearing? What is their name? Do they have any distinguishing features? Where were they last seen?

- Try to reassure the teacher that everything will be ok;

- If there is the option of using a loudspeaker system in the shopping centre, then this could be used to transmit a 'missing persons' message;

- Consider the option of using the centre's CCTV cameras to locate the missing person;

- Consider positioning a member of the security team at each exit to prevent anybody walking out with the child.

I have provided a sample response to this exercise. Before you read the sample response, use the box provided to create your own sample response, in terms of what you would ask and how you would respond.

SAMPLE RESPONSES AND ACTIONS TO EXERCISE 2:

"Hello sir, my name is Steven and I'm the customer service manager for this centre. I understand that one of your pupils has gone missing in the centre – is that correct?"

Firstly, I can assure you that the police have been called and they are on their way. I have also put a security guard at each exit to look out for the missing child. In the meantime, I would like to take some notes from you. Please can you give me a full description of the missing pupil, including their name?

Please can you tell me how long they have been missing for, and where they were last seen?" "Have you or anybody else been looking for the missing person and have you reported this to anybody else yet?

Is there a possibility that they might have wandered off to their favourite shop or gone somewhere else with another parent who was in the group?

Do you think they would understand their own name if we broadcast it over the loudspeaker system?

OK Sir, thank you for providing me with these details. This is what I propose to do. To begin with, I will check the CCTV cameras to see if we can locate the missing child. I will also brief all members of staff at the centre, including the security guards, of the missing child's description. I will put out a tannoy announcement asking the missing child to go to the nearest customer services desk where a member of staff will meet them. In addition to this, I will also put the registered nurse on standby so that she can treat the child for shock if appropriate. In the meantime, please stay here until the police arrive, as it is important that you provide them with more information. Let me reassure you that we will do everything we possibly can to locate the child. I will be taking personal responsibility for resolving this issue and I will keep you updated on progress as and when it occurs."

Sample role-play exercise 3

You are the customer service officer at a retail centre. One of the shop managers wants to see you about a gang of youths who are standing outside his shop behaving in an anti-social manner, swearing and obstructing customers from entering his shop. He is very annoyed at the situation and is losing money because potential customers are not being allowed to shop without feeling threatened.

How to prepare and possible actions to consider:

- To begin with, you should study the 'OPERATIONS' information and the 'CODE OF CONDUCT' information in the welcome pack. What do they say that relates to the above scenario? Is this kind of behaviour tolerated? Can people who behave in such a manner be escorted from the centre and should the police be involved? Can you involve the security staff or use the CCTV cameras to provide the police with evidence?

- Remember that the manager is annoyed at the situation and therefore you may have to diffuse a confrontational situation. Remember to be firm but calm, and never become confrontational yourself;

On page 123, I have provided you with a sample response to this exercise. Before you read it, use the box provided to create your own sample response. Make sure you think clearly about what questions you would ask, and how you would respond to their answers.

SAMPLE RESPONSES AND ACTIONS
TO EXERCISE 3:

"Hello Sir, thank you for coming to see me today. My name is Steven and I am the customer service officer at the centre. I understand there is an issue with a gang of youths outside your shop?

I fully understand how frustrating this must be for you, as you are losing customers. I wish to apologise unreservedly for any problems that you are experiencing at the centre. I have called the police and they are on their way. In the meantime, please can you provide me with some information about what has been happening?

How many people are there outside your shop? Has this happened before or is this the first time? Have you reported it to anyone else? Can you provide me with a description of the people who are creating the problem? What type of language are they using?

I can assure you that, in line with the code of conduct, we will not tolerate any form of anti-social behaviour and have the power to remove people from the building, as well as preventing them from re-entering at a later point. Whilst we await the arrival of the police, I will try to see if the CCTV cameras have picked anything up.

I am sorry that you have had to go through this experience Sir, but we will do everything we can to rectify the problem. As the customer service officer for the centre, it is my responsibility to ensure that you receive the highest standard of customer care. With this in mind, I will be taking full responsibility for resolving this issue and I will keep you updated of all progress as and when it occurs. Is there anything else that I can help you with?"

Sample role-play exercise 4

A customer would like to see you about an issue surrounding a dog that is in the shopping centre. She is very annoyed that a dog has been allowed to enter the shopping centre and wants to know what you are going to do about it. The dog is an 'assistance dog' for a visually impaired customer.

How to prepare and possible actions to consider:

- To begin with, you should study the 'OPERATIONS' information, the 'CODE OF CONDUCT' information and the 'EQUALITY POLICY' statement relating to the centre. What do they say that relate to the above scenario? Are 'assistance dogs' permitted? If the answer is 'yes', then the person may not have any grounds for complaint. However, it is important to listen to the complaint before responding in a calm but firm manner;

- Remember to be confident in your handling of the situation and refer to the policy of the centre for such issues. Do not get drawn into personal opinions but stick to the code of conduct for the centre and apply it accordingly.

On page 126, I have provided you with a sample response to this exercise. Before you read it, use the box provided to create your own sample response. Make sure you think clearly about what questions you would ask, and how you would respond to their answers.

SAMPLE RESPONSES AND ACTIONS TO EXERCISE 4

"Hello Madam, my name is Steven and I am the customer services officer for the centre, thank you for coming to see me today. I understand there is an issue with a dog in the shopping centre. Please would you explain what the problem is?"

"Whilst dogs are not permitted in the shopping centre, there is an exception for 'assistance dogs' like the one you have just described. Our code of conduct states that assistance dogs for the visually impaired are permitted in the centre. The centre will not discriminate against persons with disabilities and we will do everything we can to help their shopping experience to be a pleasurable one.

We have a legal requirement to allow 'assistance dogs' into the centre and if we were to ignore these rules, we would be in contravention of those laws. I am sorry Madam but in this instance I am unable to take any action. Thank you for coming to see me and have a good day."

Additional notes and guidance

- Listen to the customer's complaint and choose an appropriate moment to respond. If at any time the customer uses inappropriate or discriminatory language then you must challenge it in an appropriate manner. It is important that you ask relevant questions in order to establish the facts of the case and whether action can be taken;

- Please note that the sample scenarios provided within this guide are examples only. *They will not be the ones that you are assessed against during the assessment centre.* Whilst some of them may be similar, you must treat each case based upon the information provided and the facts surrounding the scenario. It is not the scenario that is important, but how you deal with it;

- Remember never to get annoyed or show signs of anger during the interactive exercises;

- The members of staff who are carrying out the role-plays with you, may try to make the situation difficult to deal with. They may come across in a confrontational manner during the role-play scenarios so be prepared for this. Don't let it put you on the back foot and remember that they are trying to test your ability to diffuse confrontational situations. You must remain in control at all times and treat the role actor in a sensitive and supportive manner;

- Most importantly, make sure you remember to respect equality and diversity at all times. You will be assessed in this area during every scenario;

- Challenge any inappropriate behaviour immediately during the role-play scenarios. Be firm where appropriate but do not become confrontational;

- Use keywords and phrases from the core competencies where possible;

- Finally, remember to be confident and firm whenever required. However, do respect your role as a customer service manager and provide a high level of service.

GOLDEN TIPS!

- Always try to deal with the role actor in a sensitive and support-ive manner;

- During the role-play activity phase, ask appropriate questions in order to gather information surrounding the case;

- Once you have gathered your information, you must clarify that it is all correct;

- Explain any relevant documentation in your responses. This will gain you higher marks;

- Make sensible suggestions on how you think you can improve the situation;

- Always interact with the role-play actor in a clear and construc-tive manner;

- Be sure to deal with the issues directly in accordance with the Welcome Pack and any other documentation provided.

TOP TIPS FOR PREPARING FOR THE ROLE-PLAY EXERCISES

- Learn the core competencies that are being assessed and be able to 'act' out each one;

- A good way to practice for these exercises is to get a friend or relative to 'role-play' the sample exercises contained within this guide;

- When practicing the exercises, try to pick someone you know who will make it difficult for you. You should try to resolve each issue in a calm but effective manner, in line with the core competencies;

- You may wish to purchase a copy of the 'Police Role-Play' DVD, now available at www.how2become.com.

TOP TIPS FOR PASSING THE ROLE-PLAY EXERCISES

• Use the preparation time wisely;

• Learn the pre-assessment material before you go to the assessment. This will make your life much easier;

• Remain calm during every role-play. Even if the actor becomes confrontational, it is essential that you remain calm and in control;

• If at any time during the role-play activity phase, the role-play actor uses language that is either inappropriate (including swearing), discriminatory, or uses any form of harassment, then you must challenge it immediately. When challenging this kind of behaviour you must do so in an assertive manner without becoming aggressive. Always be polite and respectful at all times;

• Use your listening skills during the role-play exercises and ask probing questions in order to gather the facts;

• Once you have gathered the facts of the case or situation, then solve the problem.

THE WRITTEN EXERCISES – REPORT WRITING

During the assessment centre, you may be asked to undertake two written exercises. Both of the written exercises will last for approximately twenty minutes each. You will be shown into the exercise room along with the other candidates in your group, and be provided with a thorough briefing before you start each exercise.

You will be provided with paper and pens, along with a 'proposal document template' on which to write your response. You'll also be given a copy of the welcome pack. During the exercise, you will be informed when there are five minutes left, and again when you have one minute left. The written exercise will be assessed after you have finished the entire assessment centre.

The following is an overview of the written exercises that you will have to carry out during your time at the assessment centre:

Written Exercise 1

In this exercise you will have to write a proposal document about issues at a fictional centre.

Written Exercise 2

In this exercise you will have to write a proposal document about an incident that happened at the aforementioned fictional centre.

When you create a written report, the assessor is looking for a well-structured, logical and relevant piece of writing. You should demonstrate a good use and understanding of grammar, and aim to make as few spelling and punctuation mistakes as possible. The written report is an area of the police officer assessment process that many people do not think they need to practice. Thus, they use their preparation time to look predominantly at the role-play and interview sections. As important as these sections are, the written report can actually gain you the highest percentage of marks out of all three of the tests. This mark could mean the difference between a pass and a fail.

On the assessment day, you will be allowed twenty minutes to read all of the information provided and create your report. This is not a lot of time, especially if you are not prepared. Therefore, it is important that you work fast and accurately. In this section, I will show you how to manage this time, so you can gather up all of the relevant information and put it together in a well-structured and logical report.

During the written assessment, you may be given a written exercise whereby you will need to take the position of a customer services officer of a retail centre. The report you are asked to create will be for the centre manager, or someone similar, based around a specific theme or scenario. When you are sent the details of your assessment date, you will also be sent two information packs – Information for Candidates and the Centre Welcome Pack (this is the centre in which you are a customer service officer). Before I move on to a sample question, and in particular how to answer it, I am going to provide you with some very important tips on how to prepare for and pass the report writing exercise.

IMPORTANT TIPS!

TIP 1! You must learn the welcome pack before you attend the assessment centre. This will make your life a lot easier during each assessment, including the report writing element. If you don't know what your role involves before you attend the assessment centre, then you are going to spend a lot of your time learning it during the actual tests! Learn it inside out before you go, in order to save time during each stage of your assessment;

TIP 2! As I have constantly stressed throughout this guide, learn the core competencies before you go to the assessment. Memorise keywords and phrases so that you can easily match them during each stage of the assessment centre;

TIP 3! In the build-up to the assessment centre, practice the sample written report exercises that you have been provided with in this guide. The more you practice, the better you will become;

TIP 4! Improve your handwriting so that it is neat and easy to read. Make the assessors life as easy as possible. Try to imagine that the person scoring your report has been marking forms for weeks on end! If they come across yours and it is easy to read, concise and flows in a logical sequence, then you are far more likely to pass.

Below is an example of the type of exercise you could be given.

SAMPLE WRITTEN EXERCISE 1

You are the customer service officer for a retail centre. Your manager has asked you to compile a report based on a new pub that is being opened in the centre. Your manager is meeting with the pub owners in a few days' time to discuss some issues, and he wants you to write a report based on the information provided. The pub owners have requested that the pub is open to serve alcoholic beverages in the centre from 11am until 11pm.

At the bottom of this page, there is a survey sheet that tells you that, on the whole, the general public and staff are not happy with the idea of a pub being opened in the shopping centre because of perceived anti-social behavioural problems, littering and rowdiness. It is your job to create a report for your manager stating what the main issues are, and what your recommendations would be.

SURVEY SHEET FOR SAMPLE EXERCISE 1

The following information has been taken from a survey that was conducted amongst 100 members of the public who regularly shop at the centre, and 30 employees who work at the centre:

- 60% of the general public and 80% of employees felt that the opening of a pub in the centre would increase littering;

- 80% of the general public and 60% of employees thought that rowdiness in the centre would increase as a result of the pub opening;

- 10% of the general public and 10% of employees thought that the opening of the pub would be a good idea.

Below we have provided you with an example of how the report could be written. You should consider the information that you have gathered, and make the recommendation(s) that you consider to be the best under the circumstances.

Remember, recommendations are suggestions for actions or changes. They should be specific rather than general.

It is important that you answer the question and state what your main findings and recommendations are, and offer a resolution.

Sample response to written exercise 1

From: The Customer Services Officer
To: The Centre Manager
Subject: New pub

Dear Sir,

Please find attached a detailed analysis of my findings and recommendations in relation to the new pub as requested. The survey conducted took into consideration the views and opinions of 100 members of the public and 30 members of staff who work at the centre.

Whilst a small proportion of staff and public (10%) felt that the opening of the pub would be a good idea, the majority of people surveyed felt that there would be problems with anti-social behaviour, littering and rowdiness. After considering all of the information provided, I wish to make the following recommendations.

The level of customer service that the centre currently provides is high and it is important that this is maintained. It is important to take into consideration the views and opinions of our customers and staff and to see things from their point of view. I believe that there would be a high risk involved if we were to allow the pub to serve alcoholic beverages from 11am until 11pm and that problems with anti-social behaviour could develop. We have a responsibility to protect the public and to ensure that they are safe whilst in the centre. Whilst it is important to initially obtain the views of the pub owners, I recommend that the pub is only permitted to serve alcoholic beverages from 11am until 1pm, and from 5pm until 7pm, so as to reduce the risk of the above problems developing.

I believe this course of action is in the best interests of the centre, its staff and more importantly, our valued customers. This alternative course of action would be for a trial period only. Providing there are no problems with anti-social behaviour, littering or rowdiness we could look to review the opening hours with a view to extending them. I am prepared to take full responsibility for monitoring the situation once the pub has been opened. I will keep you updated on my progress.

Kind regards,
The Customer Service Officer

Now that you have read the sample response, take a look at the following 5 step approach that I use when creating a well-structured report.

HOW TO CREATE AN EFFECTIVE REPORT – THE 5 STEP APPROACH

Step 1 – Read the information provided in the exercise quickly and accurately

Remember that you only have 20 minutes in which to create your report. Therefore, you do not want to spend too long reading the information. I would suggest that you spend 2-3 minutes maximum reading the information.

Step 2 – Extract relevant information from irrelevant information (main findings)

When you read the information provided in the exercise, you will notice that some of the information is of no significance. Write down which information is relevant in brief details only– these should be your main findings.

Step 3 – Decide what recommendations you are going to suggest or what action(s) you are going to take

One of the police officer core competencies is that of 'problem solving'. If asked to, then you must come up with suitable recommendations. Do not 'sit on the fence', but rather provide a logical solution to the problem.

Step 4 – Construct your report in a logical and concise manner

You are being assessed on your ability to communicate effectively. Therefore you must construct your report in a logical and concise manner. You must also ensure that you answer the question.

Step 5 – Include keywords and phrases from the core competencies in your report

During each report or letter that you construct, I strongly advise that you include keywords and phrases from the core competencies. You will notice that the 5-step approach is easy to follow. Therefore I strongly suggest that you learn and use it during the practice exercises provided later on in this section.

To begin with, let's go back to the sample response that I provided you with in the first exercise. Step 1 requires you to read the information quickly and accurately. As you have already learnt in the welcome pack, you will be aware of your responsibilities and the fact that you must provide a high level of service. Step 2 requires you to extract relevant information from irrelevant information. In order to demonstrate what is relevant, I have highlighted the key points from the report.

SAMPLE EXERCISE 1

You are the customer service officer for a retail centre. Your manager has asked you to compile a report based on a **new pub that is being opened in the centre.** Your manager is meeting with the pub owners in a few days' time to discuss a few issues and he wants you to write a report based on the information provided.

The pub owners have requested that the pub is open to serve alcohol beverages in the centre from 11am until 11pm. On the following page a survey sheet is provided, which tells you that, on the whole, **the general public and staff are not happy with the idea of a pub being opened in the shopping centre because of perceived anti-social behavioural problems, littering and rowdiness.** It is your job to create a report stating **what your main findings are and what your recommendations would be.**

<u>**So, why are the key points that I highlighted relevant? Allow me to explain:**</u>

'You are the customer service officer'

You will have already read the Welcome Pack prior to attending the assessment centre. Along with having a good idea of the duties and responsibilities required, you will also have noticed that it is your job to provide a high level of service. Therefore the report that you create needs to cater for everyone's needs. In relation to this particular situation, you must provide a solution that caters for the needs of the pub owners, the centre, members of the public, and employees.

'New pub that is being opened in the centre'

The information that you have been provided with tells you clearly that a new pub is opening in the centre. Therefore, the pub needs to operate as a business, and by doing so it needs to serve alcoholic beverages. Bear this in mind when detailing your recommendations.

The pub owners have requested that the pub is open to serve alcoholic beverages in the centre from 11am until 11pm. The pub owners have quite rightly requested that they open from 11am until 11pm, and serve alcoholic beverages throughout this period. However, you still need to provide a high level of service to everyone. Therefore you may decide to recommend a reduced opening time for a trial period only. Always look for the obvious solution to the problem. The general public and staff are not happy with the idea of a pub being opened in the shopping centre. Because the general public and staff are not happy with the idea of a pub opening in the centre, you will need to take this into account when constructing your response.

'Stating what your main findings are'

Your first task when writing your report is to state what your main findings are and what your recommendations would be. Once you have detailed the main issues, you will then need to make your recommendations based on sound judgement and common sense.

During step 3, you will need to come up with recommendations. Remember that as a police officer, you will need to solve problems based on the information and facts provided. In this particular case I have decided to offer a solution that meets the needs of all of the parties concerned – reduced opening times for a trial period with a view to extending them if all goes well. When creating your report, do not be afraid to come up with sensible recommendations or solutions.

During step 4 you will create your report. It is important that your report is concise, relevant and flows in a logical sequence. I would strongly recommend that you construct it using the following format:

Beginning:

During the introduction, provide brief details as to what the report is about. You should also provide brief details that relate to your findings. In this particular question, I am being asked to detail my main findings and recommendations. I will detail these during the beginning section of the report.

Middle:

Here you will write your main findings and recommendations. Remember to include keywords and phrases that you have learnt from the core competencies.

End:

This is the summary and conclusion. Say why you have recommended this course of action. Are there any further recommendations? If you are expecting feedback, explain how you propose to deal with this. You may also wish to state that you will take full responsibility for seeing any action through, and for keeping your manager updated on progress.

In order to demonstrate how effective this method can be, I have boxed off each section on the following page.

Creating a report using a beginning, middle and an end:

Dear Sir,

Please find detailed my findings and recommendations in relation to the new pub as requested. The survey conducted took into the consideration the views and opinions of 100 members of the public and 30 members of staff who work at the centre.

Whilst a small proportion of staff and public (10%) felt that the opening of the pub would be a good idea, the majority of people surveyed felt that there would be problems with antisocial behaviour, littering and rowdiness.

Having taken into consideration all of the information provided, I wish to make the following recommendations: The level of customer service that the centre currently provides is high, and it is important that this is maintained. It is important to take into consideration the views and opinions of our customers and staff, and to see things from their point of view. I believe that there would be a high risk involved if we were to allow the pub to serve alcoholic beverages from 11am until 11pm and that problems with anti-social behaviour could develop. We have a responsibility to protect the public and to ensure that they are safe whilst in the centre. Whilst it is important to initially obtain the views of the pub owners, I recommend that the pub is only permitted to serve alcoholic beverages from 11am until 1pm, and from 5pm until 7pm, so as to reduce the risk of the above problems developing.

I have recommended this course of action, as I believe it is in the best interests of the centre, its staff and more importantly our valued customers. This alternative course of action would be for a trial period only. Providing there are no problems with anti-social behaviour, littering or rowdiness we could look to review the opening hours with a view to extending them. I am prepared to take full responsibility for monitoring the situation once the pub has been opened. I will keep you updated on my progress.

The final step in creating your report is to use keywords and phrases which are relevant to the core competencies being assessed.

The following are sentences and phrases that I used whilst creating my report, that relate to a number of competency areas:

1. "The level of customer service that the centre currently provides is high, and it is important that this is maintained" – **relates to public service.**

2. "It is important to take into consideration the views and opinions of our customers and staff, and to see things from their point of view" – **relates to public service.**

3. "I believe that there would be a high risk involved if we were to allow the pub to serve alcoholic beverages from 11am until 11pm and that problems with antisocial behaviour could develop" – **relates to decision making and professionalism.**

4. "We have a responsibility to protect the public, and to ensure that they are safe whilst in the centre" – **relates to professionalism and public service.**

5. "Whilst it is important to initially obtain the views of the pub owners, I recommend that the pub is only permitted to serve alcoholic beverages from 11am until 1pm, and from 5pm until 7pm, so as to reduce the risk of the above problems developing" – **relates to openness to change and decision making.**

6. "I have recommended this course of action, as I believe it is in the best interests of the centre, its staff and more importantly our valued customers" – **relates to public service.**

7. "This alternative course of action would be for a trial period only. Providing there are no problems with anti-social behaviour, littering or rowdiness we could look to review the opening hours with a view to extending them" – **relates to openness to change and decision making.**

8. "I am prepared to take full responsibility for monitoring the situation once the pub has been opened" – **relates to professionalism.**

9. "I will keep you updated on my progress" – **relates to working with others.**

You can now see how important it is to learn the core competencies before you attend the assessment centre. Below I have provided you with some final hints and tips on how to create an effective report, along with a number of sample exercises to allow you to become more familiar with the application process.

IMPORTANT TIPS TO HELP YOU STRUCTURE A GOOD REPORT

- Remember that you are being assessed against your ability to communicate effectively in writing. This means creating a report that is concise, relevant, easy-to-read and free from errors;

- Make sure you answer the question;

- Aim to make zero grammar, spelling or punctuation errors. If you are unsure about a word, do not use it;

- Create your report using a beginning, middle and an end, as I have suggested;

- Use keywords and phrases from the core competencies. This is how you will be assessed;

- The amount that you write is down to you. Your focus should be on the quality of the report rather than quantity;

- Do not spend too much time reading the information and documentation provided. Spend a maximum of 3 minutes reading and digesting the documentation, and then spend at least 15 minutes writing your report. The final 2 minutes can be used for checking your report for errors.

Now that you know how to create a written report, try the sample exercises on the following pages. I have provided you with a template following each exercise for you to create your report. Don't forget to have a copy of the core competencies next to you when writing your practice reports. You will also need a copy of your welcome pack in order to respond to the questions effectively.

WRITTEN REPORT SAMPLE EXERCISE 2

You are the customer service officer for a retail centre. Your manager has asked you to compile a report regarding a number of complaints that he has received from shop owners, who state that rowdy youths are intimidating them at the centre. This is having a detrimental effect on their business, and their takings. Visitor numbers at the centre are down 25% over the last 3 months.

CCTV reports suggest that a gang of 8 youths have been circling the centre during daylight shopping hours, often approaching customers and harassing them for spare change.

The local newspaper have become aware of these incidents, and are sending a reporter to interview your manager. This interview will determine what the main problems are, and what the centre intends to do about them.

Your report should detail your main findings and also your recommendations as to how the situation can be resolved. Use the space below to create your response.

WRITTEN REPORT SAMPLE EXERCISE 3

You are the customer service officer for a retail centre. Your manager has received a request from the local council Anti-Truancy Group, who wish to patrol the centre in groups of 6 people for a 5 day period next month.

During their request, the Anti-Truancy Group has raised concerns that school children from the local area are congregating at the retail centre during school hours. CCTV cameras have confirmed these reports. In a recent report, local police have confirmed that anti-social behaviour in the area of the retail centre has increased by 15% in the last four weeks alone.

You are to create report for your manager that details your main findings and your recommendations. Use the space below to create your response.

WRITTEN REPORT SAMPLE EXERCISE 4

You are the customer service officer for a retail centre. During a recent fire safety inspection at the centre, local Fire Officers found a large number of fire escapes to be blocked with cardboard boxes that had been stored by shop owners. They also noticed that many of the areas were untidy and that the housekeeping was below an acceptable standard. Whilst the obstructions were removed, and the Fire Service will not be taking any further action, your manager is concerned that this type of incident will happen again.

He has asked you to create a report detailing your recommendations as to how this type of incident can be prevented in the future, and also how the standard of housekeeping can be improved.

Use the space below to create your response.

WRITTEN REPORT SAMPLE EXERCISE 5

As the customer service officer for a retail centre, you are required to provide your manager with a written report based on the following information.

There are 3 unoccupied shops currently at the centre. A local charity would like to use one of the shops for a 3 month period, free of charge, in order to raise money for charity by selling second-hand clothes and goods. Your manager has already conducted a survey of all shop owners and staff at the centre to see what they feel about the proposal and the results are as follows:

- *15% of shop owners support the idea;*
- *5% of shop owners do not have an opinion;*
- *80% of shop owners are against the idea;*
- *90% of staff at the centre support the idea.*

You are to create a report detailing your main findings and recommendations based on the information provided. Use the space below to create your response.

WRITTEN REPORT SAMPLE EXERCISE 6

You are the customer service officer for a retail centre. Over the last 4 weeks, the retail centre has been extremely busy and trade has been excellent. However, an issue has arisen whereby car owners are complaining that there are not enough car park spaces at the centre. Many of the shop owners are complaining that they are losing trade. This is because potential customers are turning their backs on the centre during busy periods, due to the lack of car parking spaces.

A petition has been signed by every shop owner at the centre supporting the removal of the disabled car parking spaces and real-locating them as standard car parking spaces in order to resolve the problem. There are currently 200 car parking spaces allocated at the centre specifically for disabled badge users.

Your manager is meeting with the shop owners in two days' time to discuss their proposal. He wants you to create a report detailing the main issues and your recommendations.

Use the space to create your response.

FINAL TIPS FOR PASSING THE WRITTEN EXERCISES

- In the build-up to your assessment, practice plenty of report writing;

- Improve your spelling, grammar and punctuation;

- Do not use words that you find hard to spell;

- Make sure that your handwriting is neat, tidy and legible;

- Use keywords and phrases from the core competencies;

- Construct your report in a concise manner using a beginning, middle and an end;

- Do not spend too long reading the documentation and paper-work that you are provided with. You need to allocate sufficient time to write your report or letter;

- Before you attend the assessment centre, make sure that you are fully familiar with the role of the customer services manager and all other associated documentation. There is no excuse for not learning this prior to the day.

GOLDEN TIP!

When creating your written report or letter, use the documentation provided to make suggestions as to how the situation could be improved or addressed.

I would strongly recommend that you state the reasons why you have chosen that particular course of action. Where appropriate, deal with the issue in a constructive manner and always use the correct spelling and grammar.

CHAPTER 6

Assessment Centre

Interview

As part of the PSNI assessment centre, you will usually be required to sit an interview. This interview will be done in two parts:

- The first part of the interview will be a 'get to know you' interview, with the intention of assessing your motivations and reasons for applying to the force. The interviewers are highly likely to ask you questions based around the personal statement from your original application form, so make sure you know this off by heart.

- The second part of the interview will be based around the core competencies. For example, you might have to explain how you have resolved a particular situation using the STAR method. We have outlined this method in full, on page 164. You'll need to show a clear understanding of all the requirements of the role, and demonstrate that you can use them.

Under normal circumstances, the interview board will consist of two or three people. These can be from either the uniformed side of the service or support staff. It is important to remember that whilst you will be nervous, you should try not to let this get in the way of your success. Police officers, in general, are confident people who have the ability to rise to a challenge and perform in difficult and pressurised situations. Treat the interview no differently to this. You ARE capable of becoming a police officer and the nerves that you have on the day are only natural, in fact they will help you to perform better if you have prepared sufficiently.

The crucial element to your success, as with the rest of the selection process, is your preparation. The police interview board will have a number of set questions to choose from and, whilst these are constantly changing, they will usually form part of the police officer core competencies. Before attending your interview, ensure that you read, digest and understand the police core competencies. Without these it will be very difficult to pass the interview.

During the initial stages of the interview, you might be asked questions on why you want to become a police officer, and what you know about the role.

PSNI ASSESSMENT CENTRE-INITIAL QUESTIONS

Why do you want to become a police officer?

In the build-up to your interview, you need to think carefully about why you want to become a police officer and what it is exactly that has attracted you to the role. Candidates who want to become a police officer so that they can 'catch criminals' and 'ride about in a police car with the blue lights flashing' will score poorly. Only you will know the exact reasons why you want to join the police, but here are some examples of good reasons, and examples of poor reasons.

Good reasons to give:

- To make a difference to your community, make it a safer place and reduce any fear that the public may have;

- To carry out a job that is worthwhile and makes a difference;

- The different challenges that you will face on a day-to-day basis;

- The chance to work with a highly professional team that is committed to achieving the values and principles of the force;

- The opportunity to learn new skills.

Poor reasons to give:

- The pay and pension;

- The leave or holiday that you will get;

- Wearing a uniform, which ultimately means you don't have to pay for your own work clothes;

- Catching criminals and driving a police car.

What do you know about the role?

After studying this guide, you will know a considerable amount about the role of a PSNI police officer. Remember that the role is predominantly based around the core competencies, so make sure you are familiar with them before you attend the interview. It is also advisable that you study your recruitment literature and also the website of the PSNI.

What do you know about the PSNI?

During the final interview there is a strong possibility that you will be asked questions that relate to the PSNI itself.

The following sample questions are the types that have been asked during final interviews in the past:

Q. What is it that has attracted you to the PSNI?

Q. What can you tell me about the structure of the PSNI?

Q. Can you tell me how the PSNI is doing in relation to crime reduction?

Q. What crime reduction activities is the PSNI currently involved in?

Q. What is neighbourhood policing and how does the PSNI approach it?

Q. Who are our partners and stakeholders?

In order to prepare for questions that relate to the PSNI, your first port of call is their website. From here you will be able to find out a considerable amount of information about their structure and activities and their success in driving down crime.

You may also wish to consider contacting your local police station and asking if it is possible to talk to a serving police officer about his or her role and the activities that the force are currently engaged in.

Below we have included some examples of the most common types of questions you should expect to see in the first part of your interview. We've also created some model answers to these questions, to give you a better idea of how to respond to them.

Sample question number 1

'Tell us why you want to become a police officer?'

Sample response: *"I have worked in my current role now for a number of years. I have an excellent employer, and enjoy working for them, but unfortunately no longer find my job challenging. I understand that the role of a police officer is both demanding and rewarding and I believe that I have the qualities to thrive in such an environment. I love working under pressure, working as part of a team that is diverse in nature, and helping people in difficult situations. The public expectations of the police are very high and I believe that I have the right qualities to help deliver a great service to the community. I have studied the police core competencies and believe that I have the skills to match them and deliver what they require."*

Top tips:

- Don't be negative about your current or previous employer;

- Be positive, enthusiastic and upbeat in your response;

- Make reference to the core competencies if possible.

Sample question number 2

'Why have you chosen the PSNI?'

Sample response: *"I have carried out extensive research into the PSNI, and I have been impressed by the level of service it provides. The website provides the community with direct access to a different range of topics, and the work that is being carried out through your community wardens is impressive. I have looked at the national and local crime statistics and read many different newspapers and articles. The police officers that I have spoken to have told me that they get a great deal of job satisfaction from working here."*

Top tips:

- Research the PSNI thoroughly and make reference to particular success stories;

- Be positive, enthusiastic and upbeat in your response;

- Be positive about the force and don't be critical of it, even if you think it needs improving in certain areas.

Sample question number 3

'What does the role of a police officer involve?'

Sample response: *"Prior to my application, I viewed police officers as people who simply caught criminals and worked to reduce crime. After undertaking a great deal of research, I can now see that the role of a police officer is far more diverse and varied. For example, they are there to serve the community and reduce the element of fear. They do this by communicating with their communities and being visual wherever possible. They may need to pay particular attention to a person or groups of people who are the victims of crime or hatred. Therefore the role of a police officer is to both physically and psychologically protect the community that they are serving. It is also their role to work with other organisations such as the Fire Service, Social Services and other public sector bodies, in order to reduce crime in a co-ordinated response as opposed to on their own."*

Top tips:

- Understand the police core competencies and be able to recite them word for word.

Sample question number 4

'If one of your members discussed their sexual preferences with you over a cup of tea at work, how do you think you would react?'

Sample response: *"I would have no problem at all. A person's sexual preference is their right and they should not be treated any different for this. My attitude towards them and our working relationship would not be effected in any way. I have always treated everyone with respect and dignity at all times and will continue to do so throughout my career."*

Top tips:

- Understand everything there is to know about equality and fairness. If you do not believe in equality, then this job is not for you;

- Visit the website http://www.thelgbtnetwork.org.uk.

Sample question number 5

'If you were given an order that you thought was incorrect, would you carry it out?'

Sample response: *"Yes I would. I would always respect my senior officers and their decisions. However, if I thought something could be done in a better way then I do think that it is important to put this across, but in a structured and non-confrontational manner. The most appropriate time to offer up my opinions and views would be during debrief, but I would never refuse to carry out an order or even question it during an operational incident."*

Sample question number 6

'What do you understand by the term equality and fairness?'

Sample response: *"It is an unfortunate fact that certain groups in society are still more likely to suffer from unfair treatment and discrimination than others. It is important that the PSNI and its staff strive to eliminate all forms of unfair treatment and discrimination, on the grounds that are specified in their policies or codes of practice. Equality and fairness is the working culture in which fair treatment of all, is the norm."*

Top tips:

- Try to read the PSNI policy on equality and fairness. You may be able to find this by visiting their website or asking them for a copy of it to help you in your preparation;

- Consider reading the Race Relations Act, and understand the duties that are placed upon public sector organisations such as the police.

Sample question number 7

'How do you think the police could recruit more people from ethnic minority groups?'

Sample response: *"To begin with, it is important that the PSNI continue to build effective public relations. This can be achieved through certain avenues such as the force's website or even the local press. If the Police Force have a community liaison officer, then this would be a good way to break down any barriers in the communities that we want to recruit from. Another option is to ask people from these specific groups how they view this Police Force and what they think we could do to recruit more people from their community. Along with this, it may be an option to focus media campaigns on areas where there are higher populations of ethnic minority groups."*

Comprehensive list of initial interview questions to prepare for

Q. Why do you want to become a police officer?

Q. What are your strengths?

Q. What are your weaknesses?

Q. What do you understand by the term 'teamwork'?

Q. What makes an effective team?

Q. Why would you make a good police officer?

Q. What do you think the role of a police officer entails?

Q. If you saw a colleague being bullied or harassed, what would you do?

Q. What do you think the qualities of an effective police officer are?

Q. What have you done so far to find out about the role of a police officer?

Q. Give examples of when you have had to work as a team.

Q. What would you do if a member of your team was not pulling their weight or doing their job effectively?

Q. Have you ever had to diffuse a confrontational situation? What did you do and what did you say?

Q. What are the main issues effecting the PSNI at this current time?

Q. What do you understand about the term 'equality and fairness'?

Q. What do you understand by the term 'equal opportunities'?

Q. If you ever heard a racist or sexist remark, what would you do?

Q. *Would you say that you are a motivated person?*

Q. *How do you keep yourself motivated?*

Q. *Have you ever had to work as part of a team to achieve a common goal?*

Q. *If you were in the canteen at work and two senior officers began to make homophobic comments, what would you do?*

Q. *Have you ever made a poor decision? If so, what was it?*

Q. *If you were ever given an order that you thought was incorrect what would you do?*

Q. *Have you ever had to work with somebody that you dislike?*

Q. *What is wrong with your current job? Why do you want to leave to become a police officer?*

Q. *Have you ever carried out a project from beginning to end?*

Q. *How do you think you would cope with anti-social working hours?*

Q. *Have you ever had to work shifts?*

Q. *How do you think you would cope with working the police shift system?*

PSNI ASSESSMENT CENTRE - COMPETENCY BASED QUESTIONS

The second part of the interview will last for up to 20 minutes. You will be asked four questions about how you have previously dealt with specific situations. These questions will be related to the competency areas, relevant to the role of a Police Constable, which can be found in the information pack. You will be given 5 minutes to answer each question, and will be stopped if you go over the 5 minutes. The person interviewing you may also provide you with a written copy of the question to refer to when answering. You should be prepared to answer further questions, in order to deliver a full response.

When you consider your responses to the interview questions, you should only choose examples that you feel comfortable discussing with the person interviewing you.

The interviewer will assess your responses against the type of behaviours that you will need to exhibit, whilst working as a PSNI police officer. You must make sure that you are familiar with the competencies and that your answer gives you an opportunity to explain how you have shown this behaviour. They will assess you on five different competencies during the interview. Oral Communication will be assessed throughout the interview, and you will be asked one question in relation to the following four competency areas:

- Service Delivery;

- Serving the Public;

- Professionalism;

- Working with Others.

IMPORTANT NOTE!

From time-to-time the PSNI will change the competencies being assessed during the interview. You can find the exact ones being assessed at your particular interview within the Information for Candidates documentation.

Preparing for the assessment centre interview:

When preparing for the interview you should try to formulate responses to questions that surround the assessable core competencies.

The responses that you provide should include specific examples of what you have done in particular scenarios. In your 'welcome pack', which will be sent to you approximately 2 weeks before the date of your assessment centre, you should find examples of the 'core competencies' that are relevant to a PSNI police officer. These are the criteria that you will be scored against, so it is worthwhile reading them beforehand and trying to structure your answers around them as best as you can.

For example, one of the sections you will be assessed against could be 'Working with Others'. You may be asked a question where you have to give an example of where you have worked effectively as part of a team in order to achieve a difficult task or goal. Try to think of an example where you have had to do this, and structure your answer around the core competencies required, e.g. you worked co-operatively with others, supported the rest of the team members, and persuaded them to follow your ideas for completing the task. Do not fall into the trap of providing a 'generic' response that details what you 'would do' if the situation arose, unless of course you have not been in this type of situation before.

When responding to situational questions try to structure your responses in a logical and concise manner. The way to achieve this is to use the 'STAR' method:

Situation

Start off your response to the interview question by explaining what the 'situation' was and who was involved.

Task

Once you have detailed the situation, explain what the 'task' was, or what needed to be done.

Action

Now explain what 'action' you took, and what action others took. Also explain why you took this particular course of action.

Result

Explain to the panel what you would do differently if the same situation arose again. It is good to be reflective at the end of your responses. This demonstrates a level of maturity and it will also show the panel that you are willing to learn from every experience.

Finally, explain what the outcome or result was following your actions. Try to demonstrate in your response that the result was positive because of the action that you took.

On the following page I have provided you with an example of how your response could be structured if you were responding to a question that was based around the core competency of professionalism. Remember that the following sample questions and responses are for example purposes only.

SAMPLE INTERVIEW QUESTION BASED AROUND THE CORE COMPETENCY OF PROFESSIONALISM.

'Please provide an example of where you have taken responsibility to resolve a problem?'

"After reading a newspaper appeal from a local children's charity, I decided to raise money for this worthwhile cause by organising a charity car wash for one day at the local school during the summer holidays. I decided that the event would take place in a month's time, which would give me enough time to organise things. The head teacher at the school agreed to support me during the organisation of the event and provide me with the necessary resources required to make it a success.

I set about organising the event, but soon realised that I had made a mistake in trying to arrange everything on my own. I arranged for two of my work colleagues to assist me. Once they had agreed to help me, I started out by providing them with a brief of what I wanted them to do. I informed them that, in order for the event to be a success, we needed to act with integrity and professionalism at all times. I then asked one of them to organise the booking of the school and to arrange local sponsorship in the form of buckets, sponges and car wash soap to use on the day, so that we did not have to use our own personal money to buy them. I asked the second person to arrange advertising in the local newspaper and radio stations so that we could let the local community know about our charity car wash event, which would in turn hopefully bring in more money for the charity. Following a successful advertising campaign, I was inundated with calls from local newspapers about our event, and it was becoming hard work to keep talking to them and explaining what the event was all about. However, I knew that this information was important if we were to raise our target of £500.

Everything was going well right up to the morning of the event, when I realised we had not picked up the key to open the school gates. It was during the summer holidays, so the caretaker was not there to open the gates for us. Not wanting to let everyone down, I jumped in my car, made my way down to the caretaker's house and managed to wake him up and get the key just in time before the car wash event was due to start. In the end, the day was a great success and we managed to raise £600 for the local charity. Throughout the event I put in lots of extra effort in order to make it a great success.

Once the event was over, I decided to ask the head teacher for feedback on how he thought I had managed the project. He provided me with some excellent feedback and some good pointers for how I might improve in the future when organising events. I took on-board this feedback in order to improve my skills."

Now that we have taken a look at a sample response, let's explore how the response matched the core competency.

How the response matches the core competency being assessed

In order to demonstrate how effective the above response is, I have broken it down into sections and provided the core competency area that it matches.

"...I decided to try to raise money for this worthwhile cause by organising a charity car wash day..."

Core competency matched:

- Acts with integrity;

- Uses own initiative.

"Once they had agreed to help me, I started out by providing them with a brief of what I wanted them to do. I informed them that, in order for the event to be a success, we needed to act with integrity and professionalism at all times."

Core competency matched:

- Acting with integrity and demonstrating a strong work ethic.

"...which would give me enough time to organise such an event."

Core competency matched:

- Takes ownership.

"I set about organising the event and soon realised that I had made a mistake in trying to arrange everything on my own, so I arranged for 2 of my work colleagues to assist me."

Core competency matched:

- Takes ownership;
- Uses initiative.

"...arrange local sponsorship in the form of buckets, sponges and car wash soap to use on the day, so that we did not have to use our own personal money to buy them."

Core competency matched:

- Uses initiative.

"Once the event was over I decided to ask the head teacher for feedback on how he thought I had managed the project. He provided me with some excellent feedback and some good pointers for how I might improve in the future when organising events. I took on-board this feedback in order to improve my skills."

Core competency matched:

- Asks for and acts on feedback.

"Following a successful advertising campaign, I was inundated with calls from local newspapers about our event and it was becoming hard work to keep talking to them and explaining what the event was all about. But I knew that this information was important if we were to raise our target of £500."

Core competency matched:

- Uses initiative.

"Not wanting to let everyone down, I jumped in my car and made my way down to the caretaker's house and managed to wake him up and get the key just in time before the car wash event was due to start."

Core competency matched:

- Uses initiative;
- Takes ownership;
- Showing a strong work ethic.

The explanations above have hopefully highlighted the importance of matching the core competencies that are being assessed.

When you receive your 'Welcome Pack', make sure you read it thoroughly and prepare yourself fully for the interview. Preparation is everything, and reading exactly what is required will increase your chances of success on the day.

On the following pages, I have provided you with a number of sample assessment centre interview questions that are based around the core competencies. Following each question, we have provided you with some useful tips and advice on how you may consider answering the question. Once you have read the question and the tips, use the template on the following page to create a response using your own experiences and knowledge.

SAMPLE COMPETENCY BASED INTERVIEW QUESTION 1

(Working with others):

'Please provide an example of where you have worked as part of a team to achieve a difficult task.'

Tips for constructing your response:

- Try to think of a situation where you have volunteered to work with a team in order to achieve a difficult task. It is better to say that you volunteered as opposed to being asked to show initiative and commitment;

- Those candidates who can provide an example where they achieved the task, despite the constraints of time, will generally score better;

- Consider structuring your response in the following manner:

Step 1: Explain what the situation was and how you became involved;

Step 2: Now explain who else was involved and what the task was;

Step 3: Explain why the task was difficult and whether there were any time constraints;

Step 4: Explain how it was decided who would carry out what task;

Step 5: Now explain what had to be done and how you overcame any obstacles or hurdles;

Step 6: Explain what the result/outcome was. Try to make the result positive as a result of your actions.

Now use the space on the following page to construct your own response to this question based on your own experiences and knowledge.

SAMPLE COMPETENCY BASED INTERVIEW QUESTION 1

'Please provide an example of where you have worked as a team to perform a difficult task'

SAMPLE COMPETENCY BASED INTERVIEW QUESTION 2

(Professionalism):

'Provide an example of where you have challenged discriminatory or inappropriate behaviour. What did you do and what did you say?'

Tips for constructing your response:

- Study the core competency that relates to respect for race and diversity before constructing your response;

- When challenging this type of behaviour, make sure that you remain calm at all times and never become aggressive or confrontational;

- Consider structuring your response in the following manner:

Step 1: Explain what the situation was and how you became involved.

Step 2: Now explain who else was involved, and why you felt that the behaviour was inappropriate or discriminatory. What was it that was being said or done?

Step 3: Now explain what you said or did and why.

Step 4: Explain how the other person/people reacted when you challenged the behaviour.

Step 5: Now explain what the end result was. Try to make it sound like the result was positive because of your actions.

Step 6: Finally, explain why you think it was that the people/person behaved as they did. Now use the template on the following page to construct your own response to this question based on your own experiences and knowledge.

SAMPLE COMPETENCY BASED INTERVIEW QUESTION 3

(Working with others):

'Provide an example of where you have helped somebody from a different culture or background to your own. What did you do and what did you say?'

Tips for constructing your response:

- Study the core competency that relates to respect for race and diversity before constructing your response;

- Try to think of a situation where you have gone out of your way to help somebody;

- Try to use keywords and phrases from the core competency in your response;

- Consider structuring your response in the following manner:

Step 1: Explain what the situation was and how you became involved. It is better to say that you volunteered to get involved rather than to say that you were asked to.

Step 2: Now explain who else was involved, and why they needed your help or assistance?

Step 3: Now explain what you said or did and why. Also explain any factors you took into consideration when helping them.

Step 4: Explain how the other person/people reacted to your help or assistance. Did they benefit from it?

Step 5: Now explain what the end result was. Try to make the result positive following your actions.

Now use the template below to construct your own response to this question based on your own experiences and knowledge.

SAMPLE COMPETENCY BASED INTERVIEW QUESTION 4

(Professionalism):

'Provide an example of where you have solved a difficult problem. What did you do?'

Tips for constructing your response:

• Study the core competency that relates to problem solving;

• Try to include keywords and phrases from the core competency in your response to this question;

• Consider structuring your response in the following manner:

Step 1: Explain what the situation was and why the problem was difficult.

Step 2: Now explain what action you took in order to solve the difficult problem?

Step 3: Now explain why you took that particular action, and also the thought process behind your actions.

Step 4: Explain the barriers or difficulties that you had to overcome?

Step 5: Now explain what the end result was. Try to make the result sound positive as a result of your actions.

Now use the template on the following page to construct your own response to this question based on your own experiences and knowledge.

SAMPLE COMPETENCY BASED INTERVIEW QUESTION 5

(Serving the public):

'Provide an example of where you have broken down barriers between a group of people?'

Tips for constructing your response:

- Study the core competency that relates to serving the public;

- Try to include keywords and phrases from the core competency in your response to this question, such as: "I tried to understand each person's needs and concerns." "I took steps to identify the best way that we could all work together." "I had their best interests at heart throughout." "I built confidence in them by talking to them."

- Consider structuring your response in the following manner:

Step 1: Explain what the situation was and why you needed to break down the barriers.

Step 2: Now explain what steps you took in order to achieve the goal.

Step 3: Now explain why you took that particular action, and also the thought process behind your actions.

Step 4: Explain the barriers or difficulties that you had to overcome in order to achieve the task/objective?

Step 5: Now explain what the end result was. Try to make the result sound positive following your actions.

Now use the template on the following page to construct your own response to this question based on your own experiences and knowledge.

SAMPLE COMPETENCY BASED INTERVIEW QUESTION 6

(Service delivery):

'Please provide an example of where you have organised a difficult task effectively?'

Tips for constructing your response:

• Carefully read the core competency that relates to service delivery;

• Try to include keywords and phrases from the core competency in your response to this question;

• Consider structuring your response in the following manner:

Step 1: Explain what the situation was, and what it was that you needed to organise.

Step 2: Now explain why the task was so difficult.

Step 3: Now explain what you did and why you did it. Also explain your considerations when organising the task.

Step 4: Explain what problems you had and how you overcame them.

Step 5: Finally explain what the end result was. Try to provide a positive outcome to the situation.

Now use the template on the following page to construct your own response to this question based on your own experiences and knowledge.

SAMPLE COMPETENCY BASED INTERVIEW QUESTION 7

(Professionalism):

'Tell me about a time when you changed how you did something, in response to feedback from someone else?'

Tips for creating your response:

- What did you need to develop?

- What feedback did you receive and from whom?

- What steps did you take to improve yourself or someone else?

- What did you specifically say or do?

- What was the result?

Strong response:

Police officers receive feedback from their supervisory managers on a regular basis. In their quest to continually improve, the police force will invest time, finances and resources into your development. Part of the learning process includes being able to accept feedback and also being able to improve as a result of it. Strong candidates will be able to provide specific examples of where they have taken feedback from an employer or otherwise, and used it to improve themselves.

Weak response:

Candidates who are unable to accept and use feedback from others will generally provide a weak response to this type of question. They will fail to grasp the importance of feedback and in particular where it lies in relation to continuous improvement. Their response will be generic in nature and there will be no real substance or detail to their answer.

Now take the time to prepare your own response to this question, before reading the sample response.

Sample response:

"During my last appraisal, my line manager identified that I needed to improve in a specific area.

I work as a call handler for a large independent communications company. Part of my role involves answering a specific number of calls per hour. If I do not reach my target then this does not allow the company to meet its standards. I found that I was falling behind on the number of calls answered, and this was identified during the appraisal. I needed to develop my call handling skills. My line manager played back a number of recorded calls that I had dealt with, and it became apparent that I was taking too long speaking to the customers about issues that were irrelevant to the call itself. Because I am a conscientious and caring person, I found myself asking the customer how they were and what kind of day they were having. Despite the customers being more than pleased with the level of customer care, this approach was not helping the company and therefore I needed to change it.

I immediately took on-board the comments of my line manager, and also took up the offer of development and call handling training. After the training, which took two weeks to complete, I was meeting my targets with ease. In turn, this helped the company to reach its call handling targets."

MORE SAMPLE QUESTIONS TO PREPARE FOR, BASED ON THE ASSESSABLE CORE COMPETENCIES

In this section I will provide you with a number of sample interview questions to prepare for.

SERVICE DELIVERY:

Q. Give an example of when you have worked towards an organisation's objectives or priorities?

Q. Give an example of when you have planned and organised a difficult task?

Q. Give an example of when you have carried out many different tasks at once?

Q. Give an example of when you have sought advice from others whilst carrying out a difficult work-related task?

SERVING THE PUBLIC:

Q. Give an example of when you have provided excellent customer service?

Q. Give an example of when you have addressed someone else's needs or expectations?

Q. Give an example of when you have broken down barriers amongst a group of people?

Q. Give an example of when you have worked with another person or group of people to deliver an excellent level of service?

PROFESSIONALISM:

Q. Give an example of when you have worked in accordance with an organisation's standards or ethics?

Q. Give an example of when you have taken ownership of a particular problem?

Q. Give an example of when you have acted on your own initiative to resolve an issue or difficult problem?

Q. *Give an example of when you have challenged discriminatory or inappropriate behaviour?*

Q. *Give an example of when you have acted on feedback which has been supplied by someone else?*

Q. *Give an example of when you have resolved a difficult situation in a calm manner?*

Q. *Give an example of when you have defused a potentially hostile situation?*

WORKING WITH OTHERS:

Q. *Give an example of when you have supported other members of a team?*

Q. *Give an example of when you have worked with other people to achieve a difficult task?*

Q. *Give an example of when you have briefed a team in relation to a difficult task which had to be achieved?*

Q. *Give an example of when you have persuaded a group of people to follow your course of action or plan?*

Q. *Give an example of when you have treated a person or group of people with dignity and respect?*

HOW TO IMPROVE YOUR SCORES THROUGH EFFECTIVE ORAL COMMUNICATION

Whilst you will not normally be questioned directly in relation to oral communication, you will be assessed indirectly. During the assessment centre competency-based interview, the panel will be looking to see how you communicate and also how you structure your responses to the interview questions.

Consider the following points both during the interview and whilst responding to the interview questions:

- When you walk into the interview room, stand up straight and introduce yourself. Be polite and courteous at all times and try to come across in a pleasant manner. The panel will be assessing you as soon as you walk through the door, so make sure that you give a positive first impression;

- Do not sit down in the interview chair until you are invited to do so. This is good manners;

- When you sit down in the interview chair, sit up straight and do not fidget or slouch. It is acceptable to use hand gestures when explaining your responses to the questions but don't overdo it, as they can become a distraction;

- Structure your responses to the questions in a logical manner – this is very important. When responding to an interview question, start at the beginning and work your way through in a concise manner, and at a pace that is easy for the panel to listen to;

- Speak clearly and in a tone that is easy for the panel to hear. Be confident in your responses;

- When talking to the panel use eye contact, but be careful not to look at them in an intimidating manner;

- Consider wearing some form of formal outfit to the interview such as a suit for men, and a smart dress for women. Whilst you will not be assessed on the type of outfit that you wear to the interview, it will make you come across in a more professional manner, which is how you want to be perceived.

FINAL GOLDEN INTERVIEW TIPS!

- Always provide 'specific' examples to the questions being asked;

- During your responses, try to outline your contributions and also provide evidence of the competency area that is being assessed;

- Speak clearly, use correct English and structure your responses in a logical and concise manner;

- Carry out a mock interview prior to your actual interview day;

- When answering your questions, respond to the panel as opposed to the person who has asked you the question;

- Make eye contact with all of the members of the panel as opposed to looking at just one, or worse, the floor;

- Rest the palms of your hands on your knees when you are not using them to express yourself, and keep your feet flat on the floor.

You may find some of the following phrases useful when constructing your answers:

- Dignity and respect;

- Team working and working with others;

- Strong working relationships;

- Effective team member;

- Achieving common goals;

- Customer focus;

- Public service;

- Resilient;

- Community policing;

- Sensitive to cultural issues;

- Sensitive towards racial differences;

- Presenting the right image to the public;

- Effective communication;

- Identify problems and make effective decisions;

- Motivated, conscientious and committed;

- Calm, considerate and can work well under pressure.

CHAPTER 7

Other

Assessment Stages

Once you have completed the assessment centre, you will have to wait for a decision from the PSNI on whether you have been successful. In the event that you are successful, you will be placed on what is known as 'the merit' list, and then invited to take part in five further stages.

These five stages will include:

- Medical;

- Substance Misuse Testing;

- The Physical Competency Assessment;

- Vetting;

- Online Learning.

Below we have provided you with key information that you will need to know before taking part in each of these 5 stages.

STAGE 1 = MEDICAL

The first further assessment stage you will be invited to, is the medical check. This will consist of a hearing test, an eye sight test, a BMI measurement, blood pressure and heart rate test, and some movement/flexibility tests.

Prior to the test, you'll be sent a medical history questionnaire, which you must answer with 100% honesty. It is EXTREMELY important that you fill in the whole form before the assessment day. If you bring along an uncompleted form, then you will not be assessed. You will need your GP to verify your answers, and possibly provide further information to the PSNI. If you do have any conditions, you will be expected to discuss them in further detail with your medical assessor, and bring any necessary medical letters or reports. The assessment will take approximately 1 hour to complete. Make absolutely sure that you are on time, as if you are late, then you will not be assessed.

Following your medical assessment, you will have to wait for a short period of time, before occupational health and welfare write to you directly with your result.

Presuming you are medically acceptable, you will then move onto the next stage.

STAGE 2 = SUBSTANCE MISUSE TESTING

The next stage in the process is the substance misuse test. The PSNI has introduced a policy which tests for the use of substances listed under the Misuse of Drugs Act 1971. Therefore, all applicants will need to undergo a drug screening assessment prior to being officially offered a place with the PSNI. If you test positively for the aforementioned substances, your application will be denied.

Prior to taking the test, you should be sent full details of the testing requirements and procedures.

If you are successful, you will move onto the next stage of the process.

STAGE 3 = THE PHYSICAL COMPETENCY ASSESSMENT

In order to perform successfully as a police officer in Northern Ireland, you'll need to ensure that you meet the physical requirements of the role. To assess your capability, the PSNI uses the Physical Competence Assessment (PCA). The PCA is a reflection of the day-to-day physical requirements of an officer, and involves activities such as running, climbing, lifting and weaving. These exercises are normally incorporated via an obstacle course. Along with the obstacle course, candidates will also be tested on their ability to push and pull. Both parts of the PCA will need to be completed in order for candidates to be successful.

There are five recommended training programmes which can be used to help you prepare for this assessment, which we have outlined below:

Session 1:

Run between 5km and 3 mile. Make notes on the time it takes you to complete.

Session 2:

Complete the following sequence 3 times: 1 minute of press ups, 1 minute of leg lunges, 1 minute of sit ups, 1 minute of burpees, 1 minute of rest.

Session 3:

Alternate between running as fast as possible for 2 minutes, and resting for 2 minutes.

Alternate between running as fast as possible for 1 minute, and resting for 1 minute.

Alternate between running as fast as possible for 30 seconds, and resting for 30 seconds.

Session 4:

Run, cycle or row for 3 minutes. Repeat this four times, once for each sequence.

1 minute of squats. Repeat this four times, once for each sequence.

1 minute of plank holding. Repeat this four times, once for each

sequence.

1 minute of press ups. Repeat this four times, once for each sequence.

Session 5:

Run and then jog for 1 minute each.

Run and then jog for 30 seconds each.

Run for 10 minutes at a pace which you can maintain.

If you are successful at the PCA, you will move onto the fourth stage of the process.

STAGE 4 = VETTING

This is the longest stage of the process, and can sometimes take up to 3 or 4 months to complete. Vetting involves the PSNI conducting background and security checks on you, including financial history, past convictions, educational background and contacting relatives/ previous employers to collect references. Try to be as patient as possible when waiting for this process to be completed.

STAGE 5 = ONLINE LEARNING

Once you have successfully passed the vetting process, you will be required to undertake 25 hours of e-learning material over a 4 week period. As you progress, you'll be tested on the content learned at the end of each topic. In order to progress, you will need to meet the minimum pass mark.

Once you have passed all of these stages, you will be invited to attend an induction weekend and finally will be able to enrol in college.

POLICE PROBATIONARY TRAINING:

After passing the selection process, you will undertake a long period of intensive training that is designed to help you develop into a competent police officer. First, you'll need to take part in the **Student Officer Training Programme**. This training lasts for 22 weeks in total and will require you to take shifts and work at weekends. There are 9 different locations where you might be stationed for your training. These are Garnerville, Steeple, Mahon Road, Maydown, Gough, Enniskillen, Ballykinler, Ladas Drive and Magilligan.

During your training, you will study modules in:

Justice	Crime	Traffic
Health and Safety	Community Relations	Police Relations

CODE OF CONDUCT:

During the training period, you will be observed extremely closely, both on and off duty. You should avoid getting involved in any activities which could damage your integrity in the eyes of the college, such as after hour parties, drinking or sexual relations. Furthermore, you should try to portray yourself as a liberal and middle of the road person, with no controversial opinions. If you work hard and behave like a model student, you will ultimately be rewarded.

Many of your lessons will consist of group activities and presentations. The best thing that you can do is to put yourself forward. This will show a willingness and courage to take initiative. You'll also need to be highly organised. Most lessons or tasks at the training college will require you to be present at least 5 minutes before the scheduled period, and the majority of days consist of 12 hours or more.

A large majority of candidates do not complete the training, as it is exceptionally difficult. This is deliberate. Working for the PSNI is no easy task, and you will have to be prepared to cope in really difficult circumstances. The training college further separates those who can handle the challenge, from those who can't.

If you successfully complete this training, you will be formally recognised as a constable, and then move onto your probationary period. This period will last about 2 years, and includes four more stages. During this period, you will be constantly assessed via written, practical and physical exercises.

Stage 1 = Operational Development Programme:

Stage 1 consists of an eleven week programme, which will train applicants in areas such as: Firearms, Patrolling, First Aid, Maintaining Public Order, Driving, Communications and Fire Safety. At the end of this period, officers are assigned to a district and work in a practical unit for 10 weeks.

The next 3 stages are spent back at Garnerville, completing developmental training whilst working as a day-to-day operational officer.

Stage 2 = Law procedure, and dealing with victims of crime.

Stage 3 = Law procedure, and dealing with suspects of crime.

Stage 4 = Final assessment.

Once all of these stages have been completed, officers will then be eligible to sign off on their probationary period.

CHAPTER 8

A Few Final Words...

You have now reached the end of your PSNI guide, and no doubt you feel more ready and competent to start the difficult journey that lies ahead to become a PSNI police officer. Remember that of the thousands that apply, very few actually succeed in their attempts to join the PSNI. Those people that are successful, have a few things in common:

1. They believe in themselves.

The first factor is *self-belief*. Regardless of what anyone tells you, you can become a police officer. Just like any job of this nature, you have to be prepared to work hard in order to be successful. Make sure that you have the self-belief to pass the selection process and fill your mind with positive thoughts.

2. They prepare fully.

The second factor is *preparation*. Those people who achieve in life prepare fully for every eventuality, and that is what you must do when you apply to become a police officer. Work very hard, concentrate on your weak areas and ensure you are fully aware of the entire selection process.

3. They persevere.

Perseverance is a fantastic word. Everybody comes across obstacles or setbacks in their life, but it is what you do about those setbacks that is important. If you fail at something, then ask yourself 'why' you have failed. This will allow you to improve for next time and if you keep improving and trying, success will eventually follow. Apply this same method of thinking when you apply to become a police officer.

4. They are self-motivated.

How much do you want this job? Do you want it, or do you *really* want it? When you apply to join the police, you should want it more than anything in the world. Your levels of self-motivation will shine through on your application and during your interview. For the weeks and months leading up to the police officer selection process, be motivated as best you can and always keep your fitness levels up. This will serve to increase your levels of motivation.

Work hard, stay focused and you can achieve anything that you set your mind to.